Mind Body & Spirit
Pocket Book of Days

2012

WATKINS PUBLISHING
LONDON

Mind Body & Spirit Pocket Book of Days 2012

First published in the United Kingdom and Ireland in 2011 by Watkins Publishing, an imprint of Duncan Baird Publishers
Sixth Floor
Castle House
75-76 Wells Street
London W1T 3QH

Created by One Spirit and Duncan Baird Publishers
Designed by Duncan Baird Publishers

Copyright © One Spirit 2011
Text copyright © Duncan Baird Publishers 2011
Artwork copyright © Duncan Baird Publishers 2011

All rights reserved. No part of this book may be reproduced in any form or by any electronic or mechanical means, including information storage and retrieval systems, without permission in writing from the publisher, except by a reviewer who may quote brief passages in a review.

Chief writer: Joan Duncan Oliver
Weekly exercises: Duncan Baird Publishers
Designer: Luana Gobbo
Cover artwork: Paul Zwolak
Illustrations: Nicholas Wilton, Linda Frichtel, Rachel Tudor Best, Fabian Negrin and Lydia Hess

British Library Cataloguing-in-Publication Date:
A CIP record for this book is available from the British Library

ISBN: 978-1-78028-003-5

10 9 8 7 6 5 4 3 2 1

Typeset in JensonClassico Bold, Steppin Out BT, Quadraat Sans, Chaparral Pro, Apollo MT, Nuptial, Caecilia LT Std, Trade Gothic, Joanna and Nexus Serif TF

Colour reproduction by Colourscan, Singapore
Manufactured in China by Imago

Abbreviations
BCE: Before Common Era (equivalent of BC)
CE: Common Era (equivalent of AD)

Phases of the moon:

● New moon
☽ First quarter
○ Full moon
☾ Last quarter

All dates relating to the sun signs and the phases of the moon are based on Greenwich Mean Time (GMT).

Publisher's Notes
Jewish and Islamic holidays begin at sundown on the date given. Islamic holidays may vary by a day or two, as the Islamic calendar is based on a combination of actual sightings of the moon and astronomical calculations.

Note on Public Holidays
Holiday dates were correct at the time of going to press – those indicated with an asterisk (*) were still subject to formal announcement.

Acknowledgments
The Publishers would like to thank the following for help with translations from foreign texts:
Jane Crediton, Dr. Carl Maraspini, Dr. Benedict Stolling, Rainer Wagner.

2011

JANUARY
M	TU	W	TH	F	SA	SU
					1	2
3	4	5	6	7	8	9
10	11	12	13	14	15	16
17	18	19	20	21	22	23
24	25	26	27	28	29	30
31						

FEBRUARY
M	TU	W	TH	F	SA	SU
	1	2	3	4	5	6
7	8	9	10	11	12	13
14	15	16	17	18	19	20
21	22	23	24	25	26	27
28						

MARCH
M	TU	W	TH	F	SA	SU
	1	2	3	4	5	6
7	8	9	10	11	12	13
14	15	16	17	18	19	20
21	22	23	24	25	26	27
28	29	30	31			

APRIL
M	TU	W	TH	F	SA	SU
				1	2	3
4	5	6	7	8	9	10
11	12	13	14	15	16	17
18	19	20	21	22	23	24
25	26	27	28	29	30	

MAY
M	TU	W	TH	F	SA	SU
						1
2	3	4	5	6	7	8
9	10	11	12	13	14	15
16	17	18	19	20	21	22
23	24	25	26	27	28	29
30	31					

JUNE
M	TU	W	TH	F	SA	SU
		1	2	3	4	5
6	7	8	9	10	11	12
13	14	15	16	17	18	19
20	21	22	23	24	25	26
27	28	29	30			

JULY
M	TU	W	TH	F	SA	SU
				1	2	3
4	5	6	7	8	9	10
11	12	13	14	15	16	17
18	19	20	21	22	23	24
25	26	27	28	29	30	31

AUGUST
M	TU	W	TH	F	SA	SU
1	2	3	4	5	6	7
8	9	10	11	12	13	14
15	16	17	18	19	20	21
22	23	24	25	26	27	28
29	30	31				

SEPTEMBER
M	TU	W	TH	F	SA	SU
			1	2	3	4
5	6	7	8	9	10	11
12	13	14	15	16	17	18
19	20	21	22	23	24	25
26	27	28	29	30		

OCTOBER
M	TU	W	TH	F	SA	SU
					1	2
3	4	5	6	7	8	9
10	11	12	13	14	15	16
17	18	19	20	21	22	23
24	25	26	27	28	29	30
31						

NOVEMBER
M	TU	W	TH	F	SA	SU
	1	2	3	4	5	6
7	8	9	10	11	12	13
14	15	16	17	18	19	20
21	22	23	24	25	26	27
28	29	30				

DECEMBER
M	TU	W	TH	F	SA	SU
			1	2	3	4
5	6	7	8	9	10	11
12	13	14	15	16	17	18
19	20	21	22	23	24	25
26	27	28	29	30	31	

2012

JANUARY
M	TU	W	TH	F	SA	SU
						1
2	3	4	5	6	7	8
9	10	11	12	13	14	15
16	17	18	19	20	21	22
23	24	25	26	27	28	29
30	31					

FEBRUARY
M	TU	W	TH	F	SA	SU
		1	2	3	4	5
6	7	8	9	10	11	12
13	14	15	16	17	18	19
20	21	22	23	24	25	26
27	28	29				

MARCH
M	TU	W	TH	F	SA	SU
			1	2	3	4
5	6	7	8	9	10	11
12	13	14	15	16	17	18
19	20	21	22	23	24	25
26	27	28	29	30	31	

APRIL
M	TU	W	TH	F	SA	SU
						1
2	3	4	5	6	7	8
9	10	11	12	13	14	15
16	17	18	19	20	21	22
23	24	25	26	27	28	29
30						

MAY
M	TU	W	TH	F	SA	SU
	1	2	3	4	5	6
7	8	9	10	11	12	13
14	15	16	17	18	19	20
21	22	23	24	25	26	27
28	29	30	31			

JUNE
M	TU	W	TH	F	SA	SU
				1	2	3
4	5	6	7	8	9	10
11	12	13	14	15	16	17
18	19	20	21	22	23	24
25	26	27	28	29	30	

JULY
M	TU	W	TH	F	SA	SU
						1
2	3	4	5	6	7	8
9	10	11	12	13	14	15
16	17	18	19	20	21	22
23	24	25	26	27	28	29
30	31					

AUGUST
M	TU	W	TH	F	SA	SU
		1	2	3	4	5
6	7	8	9	10	11	12
13	14	15	16	17	18	19
20	21	22	23	24	25	26
27	28	29	30	31		

SEPTEMBER
M	TU	W	TH	F	SA	SU
					1	2
3	4	5	6	7	8	9
10	11	12	13	14	15	16
17	18	19	20	21	22	23
24	25	26	27	28	29	30

OCTOBER
M	TU	W	TH	F	SA	SU
1	2	3	4	5	6	7
8	9	10	11	12	13	14
15	16	17	18	19	20	21
22	23	24	25	26	27	28
29	30	31				

NOVEMBER
M	TU	W	TH	F	SA	SU
			1	2	3	4
5	6	7	8	9	10	11
12	13	14	15	16	17	18
19	20	21	22	23	24	25
26	27	28	29	30		

DECEMBER
M	TU	W	TH	F	SA	SU
					1	2
3	4	5	6	7	8	9
10	11	12	13	14	15	16
17	18	19	20	21	22	23
24	25	26	27	28	29	30
31						

2013

JANUARY
M	TU	W	TH	F	SA	SU
	1	2	3	4	5	6
7	8	9	10	11	12	13
14	15	16	17	18	19	20
21	22	23	24	25	26	27
28	29	30	31			

FEBRUARY
M	TU	W	TH	F	SA	SU
				1	2	3
4	5	6	7	8	9	10
11	12	13	14	15	16	17
18	19	20	21	22	23	24
25	26	27	28			

MARCH
M	TU	W	TH	F	SA	SU
				1	2	3
4	5	6	7	8	9	10
11	12	13	14	15	16	17
18	19	20	21	22	23	24
25	26	27	28	29	30	31

APRIL
M	TU	W	TH	F	SA	SU
1	2	3	4	5	6	7
8	9	10	11	12	13	14
15	16	17	18	19	20	21
22	23	24	25	26	27	28
29	30					

MAY
M	TU	W	TH	F	SA	SU
		1	2	3	4	5
6	7	8	9	10	11	12
13	14	15	16	17	18	19
20	21	22	23	24	25	26
27	28	29	30	31		

JUNE
M	TU	W	TH	F	SA	SU
					1	2
3	4	5	6	7	8	9
10	11	12	13	14	15	16
17	18	19	20	21	22	23
24	25	26	27	28	29	30

JULY
M	TU	W	TH	F	SA	SU
1	2	3	4	5	6	7
8	9	10	11	12	13	14
15	16	17	18	19	20	21
22	23	24	25	26	27	28
29	30	31				

AUGUST
M	TU	W	TH	F	SA	SU
			1	2	3	4
5	6	7	8	9	10	11
12	13	14	15	16	17	18
19	20	21	22	23	24	25
26	27	28	29	30	31	

SEPTEMBER
M	TU	W	TH	F	SA	SU
						1
2	3	4	5	6	7	8
9	10	11	12	13	14	15
16	17	18	19	20	21	22
23	24	25	26	27	28	29
30						

OCTOBER
M	TU	W	TH	F	SA	SU
	1	2	3	4	5	6
7	8	9	10	11	12	13
14	15	16	17	18	19	20
21	22	23	24	25	26	27
28	29	30	31			

NOVEMBER
M	TU	W	TH	F	SA	SU
				1	2	3
4	5	6	7	8	9	10
11	12	13	14	15	16	17
18	19	20	21	22	23	24
25	26	27	28	29	30	

DECEMBER
M	TU	W	TH	F	SA	SU
						1
2	3	4	5	6	7	8
9	10	11	12	13	14	15
16	17	18	19	20	21	22
23	24	25	26	27	28	29
30	31					

Welcome to 2012

This year has special significance for many traditional cultures across the world. The Long Count calendar of the ancient Maya ends in 2012 after 5,125 years – prompting the occasional apocalyptic vision centred on 21 December, the Winter Solstice. But you needn't take disaster scenarios too seriously: Mayan experts insist 2012 isn't the end of the world – just the end of one era and the dawn of the next. Indeed, many prophetic traditions see this year as particularly propitious. We're undergoing a shift in global consciousness, they say, ushering in a more enlightened and inclusive world. If we consider that the root meaning of apocalypse isn't disaster but "uncovering the hidden", what could be more timely than to celebrate 2012 as a year of transformation?

But transformation isn't instantaneous: it's a process unfolding over time. That's where the *Book of Days* comes in. Think of it as not just an appointment diary but your trusted guide to the journey you're embarking on this year. Each month there's a different theme to focus on – an aspect of the transformation experience. You'll find practices, a project and inspirational messages to help you integrate the themes into your daily life. The year begins in January with seeding a vision of change, and ends in December with celebrating all you've achieved in 2012. The months in between support you in approaching self and world in new, more conscious and more expansive ways.

The world is us, and we are the world. Change of any magnitude, personal or planetary, starts with the individual. So turn the page – and let the revolution begin!

Plant Your Vision

It's time to seed – or feed – your vision of a more enlightened self and world. Don't fret if all the details aren't clear. Let your vision evolve as you evolve throughout the year. The first step in growing anything is to prepare the ground. Identify aspects of yourself or your life that no longer serve you, and qualities and capacities you want to nurture going forward. Leave room for fortuitous surprises.

Set Your Intention

I'm dedicated to personal transformation, and to helping create a more awake and equitable world. My guiding word is commitment.

Practice: Pulling Weeds

Negative thoughts are like weeds in a garden, robbing the soil of nutrients the flowers need to grow. Picture your mind as a beautiful garden. Your job is to tend the beds. Dig around until you isolate the weeds – fear, doubt, anger, jealousy and so on. Visualize pulling them, one by one. Once the garden is cleared, remember to tend it daily. Weed out negativity so your vision can flourish.

Project: Seeding Change

No need to start from scratch in seeding a vision. You have plenty of fertile ideas worth cultivating. But it's valuable to re-examine cherished beliefs. Look especially at those beginning "I should," "I'd never," "I've always." Ask yourself: *Is this still true for me? What does it serve? Is it time to let it go? How could I reframe it so it supports my growth?* Write down your answers for future reference.

December 26 - January 1

DECEMBER

M	TU	W	TH	F	SA	SU
			1	2	3	4
5	6	7	8	9	10	11
12	13	14	15	16	17	18
19	20	21	22	23	24	25
26	27	28	29	30	31	

JANUARY

M	TU	W	TH	F	SA	SU
						1
2	3	4	5	6	7	8
9	10	11	12	13	14	15
16	17	18	19	20	21	22
23	24	25	26	27	28	29
30	31					

FEBRUARY

M	TU	W	TH	F	SA	SU
	1	2	3	4	5	
6	7	8	9	10	11	12
13	14	15	16	17	18	19
20	21	22	23	24	25	26
27	28	29				

Monday 26

St Stephen's Day, Boxing Day
(Holiday: UK, Republic of Ireland,
Australia, New Zealand)

Tuesday 27

(Holiday: UK, Republic of Ireland,
Australia, New Zealand)

Wednesday 28

*"Do not worry if you have built your castles in the air. They are where they should be.
Now put the foundations under them."*

HENRY DAVID THOREAU (1817–1862)

Forward and back

At this auspicious time of renewal, take half an hour or so just to be quiet and project yourself twelve months into the future, to the anniversary of this moment. Imagine yourself looking back on a year of progress and change. Ask yourself what achievements you would be most proud of. Remember that, in the words of Mahatma Gandhi, "You must be the change you wish to see in the world." Start living that change now.

Thursday 29

Friday 30

Saturday 31
New Year's Eve

Sunday 1 ☽
New Year's Day

January 2 - January 8

DECEMBER

M	TU	W	TH	F	SA	SU
			1	2	3	4
5	6	7	8	9	10	11
12	13	14	15	16	17	18
19	20	21	22	23	24	25
26	27	28	29	30	31	

JANUARY

M	TU	W	TH	F	SA	SU
						1
2	**3**	**4**	**5**	**6**	**7**	**8**
9	10	11	12	13	14	15
16	17	18	19	20	21	22
23	24	25	26	27	28	29
30	31					

FEBRUARY

M	TU	W	TH	F	SA	SU
		1	2	3	4	5
6	7	8	9	10	11	12
13	14	15	16	17	18	19
20	21	22	23	24	25	26
27	28	29				

Monday 2
Holiday (UK, Republic of Ireland, Australia, New Zealand)

Tuesday 3
Holiday (Scotland, New Zealand)

Wednesday 4

"Between every two pines is a doorway to a new world."

JOHN MUIR (1838–1914)

Tree of the self

Meditate on the image of yourself as a tree. The branches are your experiences and the external influences that shape them. The trunk is your character, upright and strong, braced for all weathers. The roots are your unchanging values, which provide nourishment. Now imagine the roots of all like-minded trees intertwining in a community of spirit. This gives us self-belief, preparing the ground for the changes we seek.

Thursday 5

Friday 6
Epiphany

Saturday 7

Sunday 8

January 9 - January 15

DECEMBER
M	TU	W	TH	F	SA	SU
			1	2	3	4
5	6	7	8	9	10	11
12	13	14	15	16	17	18
19	20	21	22	23	24	25
26	27	28	29	30	31	

JANUARY
M	TU	W	TH	F	SA	SU
						1
2	3	4	5	6	7	8
9	**10**	**11**	**12**	**13**	**14**	**15**
16	17	18	19	20	21	22
23	24	25	26	27	28	29
30	31					

FEBRUARY
M	TU	W	TH	F	SA	SU
		1	2	3	4	5
6	7	8	9	10	11	12
13	14	15	16	17	18	19
20	21	22	23	24	25	26
27	28	29				

Monday 9 ◐

Tuesday 10

Wednesday 11

*"Do not be too timid and squeamish about your reactions. All life is an experiment.
The more experiments you make the better."*

RALPH WALDO EMERSON (1803–1882)

Make your own rules

We can all learn a lot from other people's experiences, but in the end the life we have is the life we create for ourselves – and there is no virtue in conforming to familiar patterns for their own sake. Originality is more valuable than conformity. Others may silently respect us or admire us, but some may follow our example. This is when we know that we have not only been true to ourselves: we have also been an inspiration to others.

Thursday 12

Friday 13

Saturday 14

Sunday 15

January 16 - January 22

DECEMBER

M	TU	W	TH	F	SA	SU
			1	2	3	4
5	6	7	8	9	10	11
12	13	14	15	16	17	18
19	20	21	22	23	24	25
26	27	28	29	30	31	

JANUARY

M	TU	W	TH	F	SA	SU
						1
2	3	4	5	6	7	8
9	10	11	12	13	14	15
16	**17**	**18**	**19**	**20**	**21**	**22**
23	24	25	26	27	28	29
30	31					

FEBRUARY

M	TU	W	TH	F	SA	SU
		1	2	3	4	5
6	7	8	9	10	11	12
13	14	15	16	17	18	19
20	21	22	23	24	25	26
27	28	29				

Monday 16

Tuesday 17

Wednesday 18

"Things alter for the worse spontaneously, if they be not altered for the better designedly."
FRANCIS BACON (1561–1626)

The habit of change

Rob change of its power to intimidate you by building small changes into your routine. Try this for a whole day, altering as much as you can. Get up an hour earlier, call an old friend for a catch-up chat, walk when you would normally drive, exchange pleasantries with the newsagent ... and so on. Make change a part of your life, so when the time comes to act on your vision, you'll be ready.

Thursday 19	Friday 20	Saturday 21
		Sun in Aquarius
		Sunday 22

January 23 - January 29

DECEMBER

M	TU	W	TH	F	SA	SU
			1	2	3	4
5	6	7	8	9	10	11
12	13	14	15	16	17	18
19	20	21	22	23	24	25
26	27	28	29	30	31	

JANUARY

M	TU	W	TH	F	SA	SU
						1
2	3	4	5	6	7	8
9	10	11	12	13	14	15
16	17	18	19	20	21	22
23	**24**	**25**	**26**	**27**	**28**	**29**
30	31					

FEBRUARY

M	TU	W	TH	F	SA	SU
	1	2	3	4	5	
6	7	8	9	10	11	12
13	14	15	16	17	18	19
20	21	22	23	24	25	26
27	28	29				

Monday 23
Chinese New Year
(Year of the Dragon)

Tuesday 24

Wednesday 25
Burns Night

*"Be still when you have nothing to say; when genuine passion moves you,
say what you've got to say and say it hot."*

D.H. LAWRENCE (1885–1930)

Halo of passion

The saint is a classic archetype of conviction – an essential quality in your wish to lead your life to the full. Call it "passion" if you prefer. The halo of passion surrounds us with an invincible aura of quiet self-belief. We may need to make sacrifices to carry out our vision – but they will always be worthwhile, for they will transport us within reach of an enriched inner life.

Thursday 26

Australia Day (Holiday: Australia)

Friday 27

Saturday 28

Sunday 29

February

Steady Yourself

A calm inner core sustains us through times of rapid change. Studies show that a centring practice grounded in meditation or prayer actually changes the structure of the brain, making us happier, kinder, more serene. It's important to find ways to maintain balance and stay connected to a spiritual source. This can be as simple as taking a few breaths and focusing inward while sitting on the bus.

Set Your Intention

I have a daily practice that centres and uplifts me. I'm awake and aware, and can handle whatever comes. My guiding word is serenity.

Practice: A Cup of Tea

Sipping a cup of tea is a meditative practice when you do it consciously. Create your own version of a formal tea ceremony. You'll want a teapot, a beautiful cup or mug, and loose tea. Select a blend that's calming: green tea is ideal. Set aside 20 minutes when you won't be disturbed. Brew the tea mindfully. As you sip it, notice the taste, the aroma, the warmth of the cup in your hand.

Project: Let the Spirit Move You

Meditating on a cushion not your style? Consider movement or music. Yoga, walking and ecstatic dance are traditional forms of moving practice, but if your God grooves to flamenco or an Afro-Brazilian beat, rock on. As for music to meditate by, favourites include chanting, singing bowls and Zen flute. But if guitar riffs are more your thing, that's OK too. Try them all until you find what moves you.

January 30 - February 5

JANUARY
M	TU	W	TH	F	SA	SU
						1
2	3	4	5	6	7	8
9	10	11	12	13	14	15
16	17	18	19	20	21	22
23	24	25	26	27	28	29
30	31					

FEBRUARY
M	TU	W	TH	F	SA	SU
		1	2	3	4	5
6	7	8	9	10	11	12
13	14	15	16	17	18	19
20	21	22	23	24	25	26
27	28	29				

MARCH
M	TU	W	TH	F	SA	SU
		1	2	3	4	5
5	6	7	8	9	10	11
12	13	14	15	16	17	18
19	20	21	22	23	24	25
26	27	28	29	30	31	

Monday 30

Tuesday 31 ◐

Wednesday 1

"The body is a big sagacity, a plurality with one sense, a war and a peace, a flock and a shepherd."

FRIEDRICH NIETZSCHE (1844–1900)

Solomon's Seal

The six-pointed star of overlapping triangles, known as the Star of David or Solomon's Seal, was seen by the psychologist Carl Jung and his followers as a symbol of the union of opposites – the personal, temporary world of the ego fused with the universal, timeless world of the non-ego. By acknowledging and accepting this opposition within our being, we move one step nearer to awareness and fulfilment.

Thursday 2

Candlemas
Brigit (Imbloc)

Friday 3

Saturday 4

Sunday 5

February 6 – February 12

JANUARY

M	TU	W	TH	F	SA	SU
						1
2	3	4	5	6	7	8
9	10	11	12	13	14	15
16	17	18	19	20	21	22
23	24	25	26	27	28	29
30	31					

FEBRUARY

M	TU	W	TH	F	SA	SU
		1	2	3	4	5
6	**7**	**8**	**9**	**10**	**11**	**12**
13	14	15	16	17	18	19
20	21	22	23	24	25	26
27	28	29				

MARCH

M	TU	W	TH	F	SA	SU
		1	2	3	4	
5	6	7	8	9	10	11
12	13	14	15	16	17	18
19	20	21	22	23	24	25
26	27	28	29	30	31	

Monday 6

Waitangi Day
(Holiday: New Zealand)

Tuesday 7

Wednesday 8

"Meditation fosters wisdom; lack of meditation leaves ignorance. Know well what takes you forward and what holds you back, and choose the path that leads to wisdom."

THE BUDDHA (c.563– c.483 BCE)

Wind and mind

Sit comfortably by a window on a windy day and "adopt" the wind as your spirit companion. Imagine you have harnessed its energy and you are making those clouds move across the sky or those branches shake on their tree, by "telekinesis" (mind power). This is an effective quick-fix meditation, distracting the mind from its habitual swirl of random thoughts. It is also a vivid reminder of the limitless power of the imagination.

Thursday 9

Friday 10

Saturday 11

Sunday 12

February 13 – February 19

JANUARY
M	TU	W	TH	F	SA	SU
						1
2	3	4	5	6	7	8
9	10	11	12	13	14	15
16	17	18	19	20	21	22
23	24	25	26	27	28	29
30	31					

FEBRUARY
M	TU	W	TH	F	SA	SU
	1	2	3	4	5	
6	7	8	9	10	11	12
13	**14**	**15**	**16**	**17**	**18**	**19**
20	21	22	23	24	25	26
27	28	29				

MARCH
M	TU	W	TH	F	SA	SU
		1	2	3	4	5
5	6	7	8	9	10	11
12	13	14	15	16	17	18
19	20	21	22	23	24	25
26	27	28	29	30	31	

Monday 13

Tuesday 14
St. Valentine's Day

Wednesday 15

"We may quarrel with men about things on Earth, but we never quarrel about the Great Spirit."

CHIEF JOSEPH, NEZ PIERCE (1840–1904)

Your virtual clan

The Pacific Northwest Indians traditionally used the totem pole as a celebration of clanhood or kinship. But kinship did not just mean blood ties: people were also believed to be related to each other by experience and by bravery. Identify ten members of your clan, in this extended sense, excluding family. Some might even be historical figures. Draw strength and resolve from what you share with these individuals.

Thursday 16

Friday 17

Saturday 18

Sunday 19

February 20 - February 26

JANUARY

M	TU	W	TH	F	SA	SU
						1
2	3	4	5	6	7	8
9	10	11	12	13	14	15
16	17	18	19	20	21	22
23	24	25	26	27	28	29
30	31					

FEBRUARY

M	TU	W	TH	F	SA	SU
		1	2	3	4	5
6	7	8	9	10	11	12
13	14	15	16	17	18	19
20	**21**	**22**	**23**	**24**	**25**	**26**
27	28	29				

MARCH

M	TU	W	TH	F	SA	SU
		1	2	3	4	5
6	7	8	9	10	11	12
13	14	15	16	17	18	19
20	21	22	23	24	25	26
27	28	29	30	31		

Monday 20
Sun in Pisces

Tuesday 21 ●
Shrove Tuesday

Wednesday 22
Ash Wednesday
Tibetan New Year (Losar)

"Nirvana is not the blowing out of the candle. It is the extinguishing of the flame because day is come."

RABINDRANATH TAGORE (1861–1941)

No one self

Buddhism teaches the notion of *anatta* or non-self: there is no unchanging core of the self we can point to and say, "Here I am." Instead, our body and mind, our feelings, our perceptions and our mental formations (including intention and emotions) combine in a complex pattern of activity, and out of this arises our consciousness. By letting go of the idea of self, we can shed our attachments to sensations and to habits and reach awareness.

Thursday 23

Friday 24

Saturday 25

Sunday 26

March

Listen to Your Body

"The body never lies," health gurus tell us, but what exactly is yours saying? We all know that proper sleep, exercise and nutrition are essential energy-builders. But don't forget emotional and environmental factors. Anything from air quality to mercury levels in seafood to a gossipy neighbour can weigh on your health and well-being. And watch what words and images you expose your mind to: violence is toxic.

Set Your Intention

I honour my body by giving it the nutrients, exercise and rest it needs.
I seek out life-affirming people and media. My guiding word is balance.

Practice: Put Your Foot Down

Facing change confidently calls for strong feet. A firm stance allows you to hold your ground and walk resolutely into the future. Pamper your feet with pedicures and regular chiropodist visits. Massage pressure points with a wooden roller or tennis ball. Metaphysically, feet represent what you stand for. While soaking yours in warm scented water, reflect on your commitment to truth and strength.

Project: Go Vegan . . . or Flexitarian

Scan a list of famous vegetarians and vegans: you may never touch meat again. If you're not there yet, try going "flexitarian" – more veggies, sustainable seafood, local produce – or be vegan by day, anything goes at dinner. Find a food writer or TV chef who inspires you – someone who can make a meal of ingredients like curried cauliflower and stuffed squash blossoms. For your health and the planet's, ease into raw foods.

February 27 - March 4

FEBRUARY

M	TU	W	TH	F	SA	SU
	1	2	3	4	5	
6	7	8	9	10	11	12
13	14	15	16	17	18	19
20	21	22	23	24	25	26
27	28	29				

MARCH

M	TU	W	TH	F	SA	SU
			1	2	3	4
5	6	7	8	9	10	11
12	13	14	15	16	17	18
19	20	21	22	23	24	25
26	27	28	29	30	31	

APRIL

M	TU	W	TH	F	SA	SU
						1
2	3	4	5	6	7	8
9	10	11	12	13	14	15
16	17	18	19	20	21	22
23	24	25	26	27	28	29
30						

Monday 27

Tuesday 28

Wednesday 29

"Health is a state of complete physical, mental and social well-being, and not merely the absence of disease or infirmity."

WORLD HEALTH ORGANIZATION (1948)

Quick fix

If you feel the need for a mid-morning snack, or you find yourself having to snack in the afternoon because you've been too busy for lunch, choose foods with a low glycemic index (GI): they will release their energy more slowly and steadily, so that you feel full for longer and end up consuming fewer calories without feeling hungry. Oakcakes, bananas, nuts and dried apricots are all good options.

Thursday 1

St David's Day

Friday 2

Saturday 3

Sunday 4

March 5 - March 11

FEBRUARY

M	TU	W	TH	F	SA	SU
		1	2	3	4	5
6	7	8	9	10	11	12
13	14	15	16	17	18	19
20	21	22	23	24	25	26
27	28	29				

MARCH

M	TU	W	TH	F	SA	SU
		1	2	3	4	
5	6	7	8	9	10	11
12	13	14	15	16	17	18
19	20	21	22	23	24	25
26	27	28	29	30	31	

APRIL

M	TU	W	TH	F	SA	SU
					1	
2	3	4	5	6	7	8
9	10	11	12	13	14	15
16	17	18	19	20	21	22
23	24	25	26	27	28	29
30						

Monday 5
Labour Day (Western Australia)

Tuesday 6

Wednesday 7
Purim begins at sundown

"Lack of activity undermines the good condition of every human being, while movement and methodical physical exercise save and preserve it."

PLATO (427–347 BCE)

Starfish wiggle

When you are feeling stressed or physically tense, try the "starfish wiggle" as a quick-fix solution. Stand upright in loose clothing and imagine yourself in the horizontal dimension rather than the vertical. Think of yourself as a five-pointed starfish – your head, plus four limbs. Shake around all five appendages slowly and loosely, one after the other, as if trying to attract the attention of a nearby starfish. This should eliminate some of your tensions.

Thursday 8

International Women's Day

Friday 9

Saturday 10

Sunday 11

March 12 - March 18

FEBRUARY

M	TU	W	TH	F	SA	SU
			1	2	3	4	5
6	7	8	9	10	11	12
13	14	15	16	17	18	19
20	21	22	23	24	25	26
27	28	29				

MARCH

M	TU	W	TH	F	SA	SU
		1	2	3	4	
5	6	7	8	9	10	11
12	**13**	**14**	**15**	**16**	**17**	**18**
19	20	21	22	23	24	25
26	27	28	29	30	31	

APRIL

M	TU	W	TH	F	SA	SU
					1	
2	3	4	5	6	7	8
9	10	11	12	13	14	15
16	17	18	19	20	21	22
23	24	25	26	27	28	29
30						

Monday 12

Labour Day (Tasmania, Victoria)
Commonweath Day

Tuesday 13

Wednesday 14

"Health and good estate of body are above all gold, and a strong body above infinite wealth."

ECCLESIASTES 30:15

Palace of intention

Use mind power to help you overcome gym phobia. Imagine you belong to a super-fit élite, whose members are so concentrated on physical development that they don't care a jot what everyone else looks like. If people do look at you in the gym, it's because they admire your determination. Your aim may be to tone the body, but that doesn't mean judging yourself on your appearance – only on the quality of your intention.

Thursday 15

Friday 16

Saturday 17
St Patrick's Day (Holiday: Northern Ireland, Republic of Ireland)

Sunday 18
Mother's Day (UK)

March 19 – March 25

FEBRUARY

M	TU	W	TH	F	SA	SU
	1	2	3	4	5	
6	7	8	9	10	11	12
13	14	15	16	17	18	19
20	21	22	23	24	25	26
27	28	29				

MARCH

M	TU	W	TH	F	SA	SU
			1	2	3	4
5	6	7	8	9	10	11
12	13	14	15	16	17	18
19	**20**	**21**	**22**	**23**	**24**	**25**
26	27	28	29	30	31	

APRIL

M	TU	W	TH	F	SA	SU
						1
2	3	4	5	6	7	8
9	10	11	12	13	14	15
16	17	18	19	20	21	22
23	24	25	26	27	28	29
30						

Monday 19

Tuesday 20
Spring Equinox

Wednesday 21
Sun in Aries

"Reason is our soul's left hand, Faith her right."

JOHN DONNE (1572–1631)

Pressure point

Perform this simple acupressure technique to stimulate your awareness. Hold your left hand, palm down with the thumb and the forefinger spread, in front of you, held from beneath by your right hand. Apply gentle pressure with your right thumb to the fleshy part of your left hand between the thumb and the forefinger. Hold this position for exactly two minutes. Then change hands and repeat the procedure.

Thursday 22

Friday 23

Saturday 24

Sunday 25
British Summer Time begins

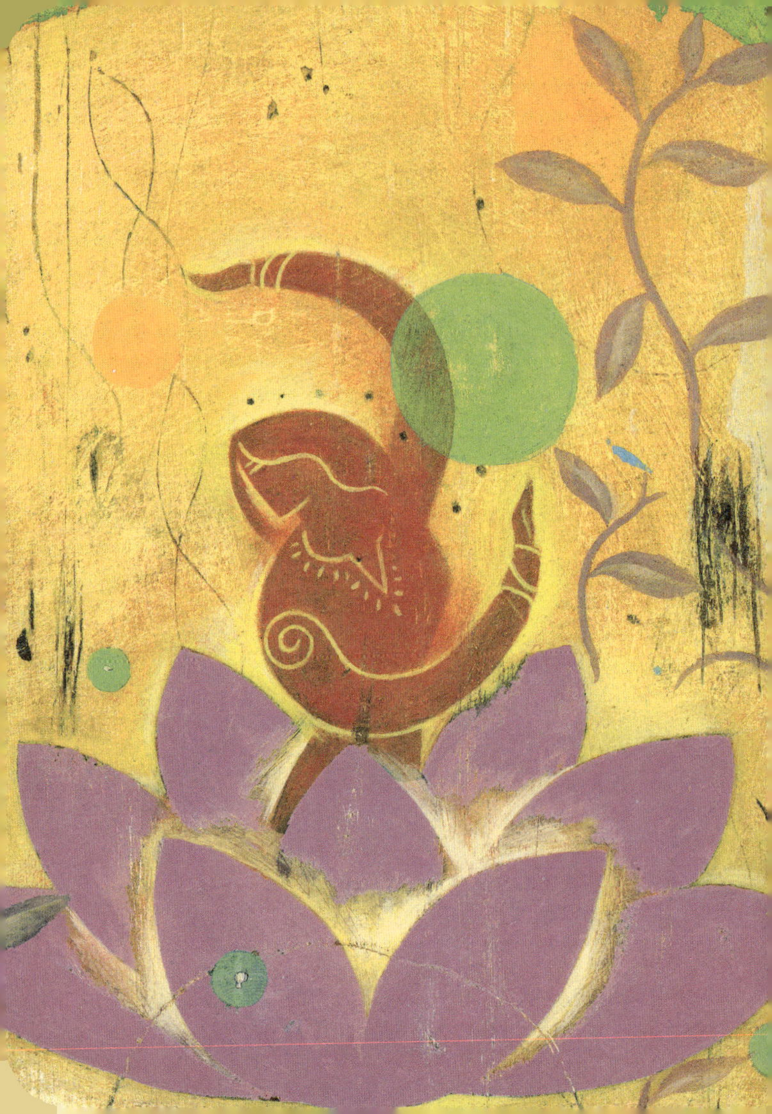

April

Live in Harmony

Fast food restaurants know that the colour orange makes you eat more. Our surroundings influence our well-being – not to mention our productivity and adaptability to change. To create an environment for happiness and success, clear and beautify your home and workspace. Make sure they express who you're becoming, not who you were. Worn or broken furnishings are like outdated attitudes that fix us in the past.

Set Your Intention

My home and workspace reflect who I am, and support change and growth in my life. I surround myself with beauty. My guiding word is comfort.

Practice: Flower Power

You don't have to be a master of Ikebana – Zen flower arranging – to have a meditative experience placing flowers in a vase. Even the simplest arrangement can be a sacred offering expressing a reverence for nature and a peaceful heart. Traditional Ikebana is very stylized. But why not be more freewheeling? A single bloom in a beautiful container can be as pleasing as any formal arrangement.

Project: House Healing

Whether your home suffers from bad energy, creepy crawlies or too much dust, a house healing may be in order. Leave bug problems to the pros, but the rest is DIY. Step one: scrub, vacuum and polish till the place gleams. Open the windows. Then smudge with sage or incense to clear negative vibes. Finish by inviting in positive energy: light a candle and say a blessing: "May love and joy fill this home."

March 26 - April 1

MARCH
M	TU	W	TH	F	SA	SU
			1	2	3	4
5	6	7	8	9	10	11
12	13	14	15	16	17	18
19	20	21	22	23	24	25
26	27	28	29	30	31	

APRIL
M	TU	W	TH	F	SA	SU
						1
2	3	4	5	6	7	8
9	10	11	12	13	14	15
16	17	18	19	20	21	22
23	24	25	26	27	28	29
30						

MAY
M	TU	W	TH	F	SA	SU
1	2	3	4	5	6	7
8	9	10	11	12	13	14
15	16	17	18	19	20	21
22	23	24	25	26	27	28
29	30	31				

Monday 26

Tuesday 27

Wednesday 28

"There is a magic in that little word, home; it is a mystic circle tht surrounds comforts and virtues, never known beyond its hallowed limits."

ROBERT SOUTHEY (1774–1843)

Spring cleaning

Thoroughly cleaning the house on the first warm day of spring is a tradition in many countries with a cold winter. Follow this practice and devote at least a few days to the project. This gives you the chance to throw away clutter, replace or mend whatever is broken and make the home a more pleasant place to live – as well as providing a motivating counterpart to the broader changes you plan to make within your life over the coming months.

Thursday 29

Friday 30

Saturday 31

Sunday 1

April Fool's Day
Palm Sunday

April 2 - April 8

MARCH
M	TU	W	TH	F	SA	SU
			1	2	3	4
5	6	7	8	9	10	11
12	13	14	15	16	17	18
19	20	21	22	23	24	25
26	27	28	29	30	31	

APRIL
M	TU	W	TH	F	SA	SU
						1
2	3	4	5	6	7	8
9	10	11	12	13	14	15
16	17	18	19	20	21	22
23	24	25	26	27	28	29
30						

MAY
M	TU	W	TH	F	SA	SU
	1	2	3	4	5	6
7	8	9	10	11	12	13
14	15	16	17	18	19	20
21	22	23	24	25	26	27
28	29	30	31			

Monday 2

Tuesday 3

Wednesday 4

"The best of us is like water. Water is good. It benefits all things and competes with none. It dwells in humble places that people disdain. That is why water is so near to the Tao."

LAO TZU (6TH CENTURY BCE)

Cultivate simplicity

Take inspiration from Taoism and aim to live in simplicity (*pu*) – in a place where you are happy at times just to be, following the principle of non-action (*wu wei*). Finding the pure self within is easier in surroundings stripped down to their essentials, with perhaps a few focal points that remind us of the beauty of the spirit (a Buddha or Shiva statue) and the beauty of nature (a piece of driftwood or a sprig of blossom).

Thursday 5

Friday 6

Good Friday (Holiday: UK, Australia, New Zealand)
Passover (Pesach) begins at sundown

Saturday 7
Easter Saturday (Holiday: Australia, excluding W. Australia and Tasmania)

Sunday 8

April 9 - April 15

MARCH
M	TU	W	TH	F	SA	SU
			1	2	3	4
5	6	7	8	9	10	11
12	13	14	15	16	17	18
19	20	21	22	23	24	25
26	27	28	29	30	31	

APRIL
M	TU	W	TH	F	SA	SU
						1
2	3	4	5	6	7	8
9	10	11	12	13	14	15
16	17	18	19	20	21	22
23	24	25	26	27	28	29
30						

MAY
M	TU	W	TH	F	SA	SU
	1	2	3	4	5	6
7	8	9	10	11	12	13
14	15	16	17	18	19	20
21	22	23	24	25	26	27
28	29	30	31			

Monday 9
Easter Monday (Holiday: UK, excluding Scotland; Republic of Ireland, Australia, New Zealand)

Tuesday 10
Easter Tuesday (Holiday: Tasmania)

Wednesday 11

"With an eye made quiet by the power of harmony, and the deep power of joy, we see into the life of things."

WILLIAM WORDSWORTH (1770–1850)

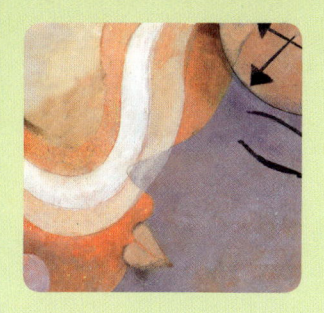

Feng Shui bedtime

Remodel your bedroom on Feng Shui principles. Ensure that the foot of the bed does not face a door or window – if it has to, place a dressing table or chest of drawers at the end of it. Create a four-poster effect to make a protective energy envelope around the bed. Opt for a solid wooden headboard if practicable. Use pale, pastel or dark colours, rather than mid-tones, to enhance yin energy and quieten the feel of the room.

Thursday 12

Friday 13 ☾

Saturday 14

Sunday 15

April 16 - April 22

MARCH

M	TU	W	TH	F	SA	SU
			1	2	3	4
5	6	7	8	9	10	11
12	13	14	15	16	17	18
19	20	21	22	23	24	25
26	27	28	29	30	31	

APRIL

M	TU	W	TH	F	SA	SU
						1
2	3	4	5	6	7	8
9	10	11	12	13	14	15
16	**17**	**18**	**19**	**20**	**21**	**22**
23	24	25	26	27	28	29
30						

MAY

M	TU	W	TH	F	SA	SU
	1	2	3	4	5	6
7	8	9	10	11	12	13
14	15	16	17	18	19	20
21	22	23	24	25	26	27
28	29	30	31			

Monday 16

Tuesday 17

Wednesday 18

"Music is a higher revelation than all wisdom and philosophy.
Music is the electrical soil in which the spirit lives, thinks, and invents."

LUDWIG VAN BEETHOVEN (1770–1827)

Healing music

Klezmer music has its roots in Eastern Europe, where itinerant Jewish troubadours celebrated social events such as weddings. With its distinctive shades of gypsy music and jazz, it expresses a whole range of emotions from the joy of union to the melancholy of parting. Fill your home with klezmer. Find a piece that echoes your mood – dance or reflect, according to circumstances. Or just dance – it can have a healing effect when you are feeling blue.

Thursday 19

Friday 20

Saturday 21
Sun in Taurus

Sunday 22
Earth Day

April 23 - April 29

MARCH

M	TU	W	TH	F	SA	SU
			1	2	3	4
5	6	7	8	9	10	11
12	13	14	15	16	17	18
19	20	21	22	23	24	25
26	27	28	29	30	31	

APRIL

M	TU	W	TH	F	SA	SU
						1
2	3	4	5	6	7	8
9	10	11	12	13	14	15
16	17	18	19	20	21	22
23	**24**	**25**	**26**	**27**	**28**	**29**
30						

MAY

M	TU	W	TH	F	SA	SU
	1	2	3	4	5	6
7	8	9	10	11	12	13
14	15	16	17	18	19	20
21	22	23	24	25	26	27
28	29	30	31			

Monday 23

St George's Day

Tuesday 24

Wednesday 25

Anzac Day (Holiday: Australia, New Zealand)

"There is nothing you can see that is not a flower; there is nothing you can think that is not the moon."

MATSUO BASHO (1644–1694)

Sacred scents

Incense is burned in sacred spaces in several religions – the biblical book of Exodus (30: 34–38) has instructions on this. Burn incense as you meditate and note the effect on your state of mind. You may well gain significantly in peace and awareness. For relaxation, try cinnamon or sandalwood; for a calmer, clearer mind, try juniper or sage; or to brighten a dark mood, experiment with frankincense.

Thursday 26

Friday 27

Saturday 28

Sunday 29 ☽

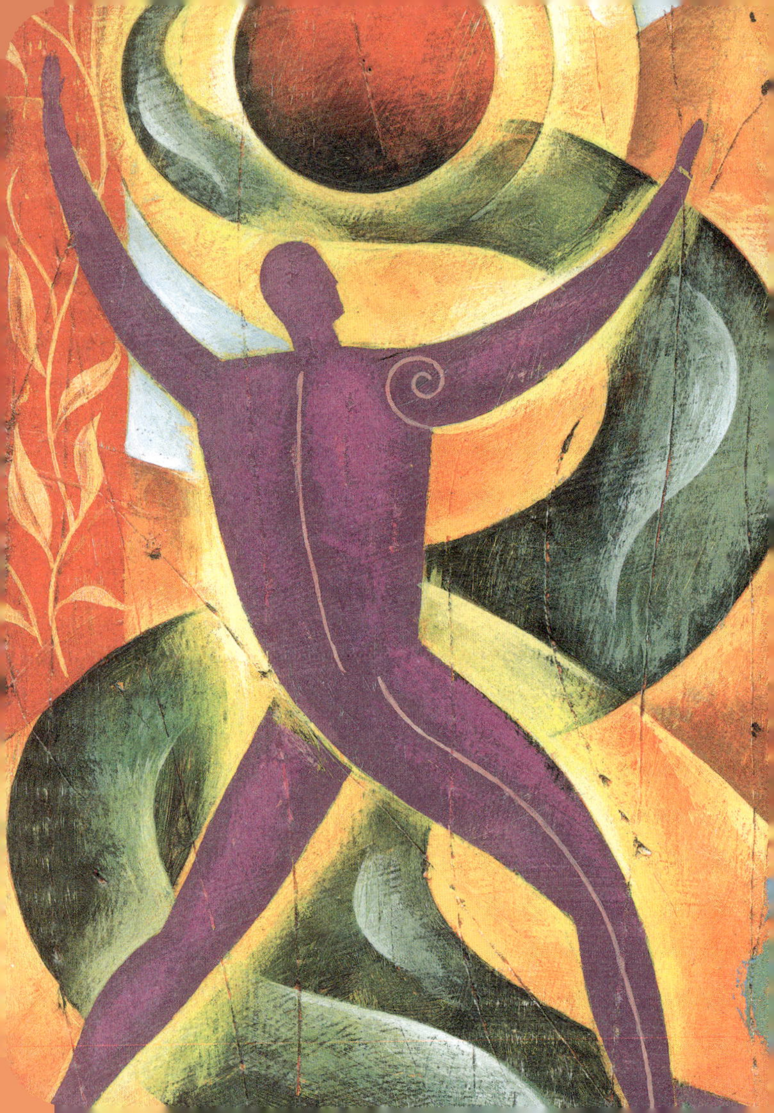

May

Consume Consciously

Wasteful consumption is destroying the Earth, and is expensive and time-intensive to maintain. Work out how to spend your resources wisely and create a sustainable lifestyle. Consuming consciously isn't just a matter of switching to jute shopping bags and public transport. It's about refining your values, rechannelling your shopping urge, and reducing your possessions to only what you use and love.

Set Your Intention

I'm acquiring less, re-using what I have and recycling what I discard.
My guiding words are "less is more."

Practice: Zen Weekend

Eat like a Zen monk for a weekend. Plan your menu and shopping so that by Sunday night you've consumed every bit of food you bought. Use fish left from dinner as a lunchtime sandwich filler. Leftover veggies can make a soup for supper, and with brown rice or millet, another entrée. You get the idea. By the end of the weekend, you'll be feeling virtuous – and amazed at how little it takes to eat well.

Project: Wardrobe Diet

Wardrobe crammed with clothes you never wear? Take up one of the challenges floating around the Webiverse. Pick six pieces of clothing and wear only those for a month. (Shoes, underwear and accessories don't count.) If that notion sends your sartorial self into shock, allow yourself 30 items. OK, 40. At month's end see if you don't think Socrates had a point when he said, "How many things I can do without!"

April 30 – May 6

APRIL

M	TU	W	TH	F	SA	SU
						1
2	3	4	5	6	7	8
9	10	11	12	13	14	15
16	17	18	19	20	21	22
23	24	25	26	27	28	29
30						

MAY

M	TU	W	TH	F	SA	SU
	1	2	3	4	5	6
7	8	9	10	11	12	13
14	15	16	17	18	19	20
21	22	23	24	25	26	27
28	29	30	31			

JUNE

M	TU	W	TH	F	SA	SU
				1	2	3
4	5	6	7	8	9	10
11	12	13	14	15	16	17
18	19	20	21	22	23	24
25	26	27	28	29	30	31

Monday 30

Tuesday 1
Beltane

Wednesday 2

"When you put your hand into a flowing stream, you touch the last that has gone before and the first of what is still to come."

LEONARDO DA VINCI (1452–1519)

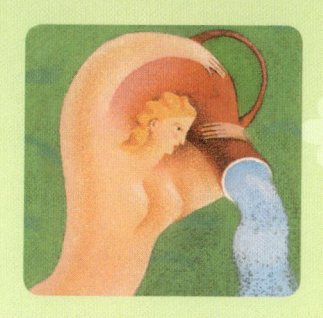

Rain harvest

Only half the people in the world have clean water at their fingertips. Treat water like the precious commodity it is. Ensure that you catch rainwater – as much as you can. Buy a water butt and use it not only for watering garden and house plants but also for rinsing the car or hosing down the patio. Only boil as much water in the kettle as you will need. When it rains, give thanks, collect a bowlful and wash your hands and face like a true child of nature.

Thursday 3

Friday 4

Saturday 5

Sunday 6

May 7 - May 13

APRIL
M	TU	W	TH	F	SA	SU
						1
2	3	4	5	6	7	8
9	10	11	12	13	14	15
16	17	18	19	20	21	22
23	24	25	26	27	28	29
30						

MAY
M	TU	W	TH	F	SA	SU
	1	2	3	4	5	6
7	8	9	10	11	12	13
14	15	16	17	18	19	20
21	22	23	24	25	26	27
28	29	30	31			

JUNE
M	TU	W	TH	F	SA	SU
				1	2	3
4	5	6	7	8	9	10
11	12	13	14	15	16	17
18	19	20	21	22	23	24
25	26	27	28	29	30	31

Monday 7
May Holiday (UK, Republic of Ireland)
Labour Day (Queensland)

Tuesday 8

Wednesday 9

"Each blade of grass has its spot on Earth whence it draws its life, its strength; and so is man rooted to the land from which he draws his faith together with his life."

JOSEPH CONRAD (1857–1924)

The law of proximity

A "locavore" is someone who restricts their diet as much as possible to produce grown locally. Set your own limit – for example, a radius of 100 miles. Food that travels vast distances clocks up food miles and increases carbon emissions. Eating local produce brings you into contact with producers. To make that vital connection between food and people at the supply side, as well as the demand side, is to be more grounded and more eco-aware.

Thursday 10

Friday 11

Saturday 12

Sunday 13

Mother's Day (Australia, New Zealand)

May 14 - May 20

APRIL
M	TU	W	TH	F	SA	SU
						1
2	3	4	5	6	7	8
9	10	11	12	13	14	15
16	17	18	19	20	21	22
23	24	25	26	27	28	29
30						

MAY
M	TU	W	TH	F	SA	SU
	1	2	3	4	5	6
7	8	9	10	11	12	13
14	**15**	**16**	**17**	**18**	**19**	**20**
21	22	23	24	25	26	27
28	29	30	31			

JUNE
M	TU	W	TH	F	SA	SU
				1	2	3
4	5	6	7	8	9	10
11	12	13	14	15	16	17
18	19	20	21	22	23	24
25	26	27	28	29	30	

Monday 14

Tuesday 15

Wednesday 16

"There is no need for temples, no need for complicated philosophy.
Our own brain, our own heart is our temple; the philosophy is kindness."

H.H. THE DALAI LAMA (B. 1935)

Eco mandala

Meditate on the mandala depicted here – a schematic image of our beloved planet, with its four traditional elements, all protected within a circle of universal virtue. The four projecting leaves represent peace, love, harmony and wisdom. So long as we invest maximum energy into these values, we improve our chances of keeping the world a fit place for civilization. Take the mandala into your heart and live by its simple wisdom.

Thursday 17

Ascension Day

Friday 18

Saturday 19

Sunday 20

May 21 - May 27

APRIL

M	TU	W	TH	F	SA	SU
						1
2	3	4	5	6	7	8
9	10	11	12	13	14	15
16	17	18	19	20	21	22
23	24	25	26	27	28	29
30						

MAY

M	TU	W	TH	F	SA	SU
	1	2	3	4	5	6
7	8	9	10	11	12	13
14	15	16	17	18	19	20
21	22	23	24	25	26	27
28	29	30	31			

JUNE

M	TU	W	TH	F	SA	SU
				1	2	3
4	5	6	7	8	9	10
11	12	13	14	15	16	17
18	19	20	21	22	23	24
25	26	27	28	29	30	

Monday 21
Victoria Day (Canada)

Tuesday 22
Sun in Gemini

Wednesday 23

"You can owe nothing, if you give back its light to the sun."

ANTONIO PORCHIA (1885–1968)

Solar gifts

The sun is a symbol of infinite love and generosity, but also a very literal source of worldly energy that can be harnessed. Buy into solar power – the energy of the future. If you can't afford a solar panel for your home or for your pool, at least acquire a solar device for charging your mobile phone or radio. Connect with the sun, the bountiful giver of all we enjoy. This is the great symbolic miracle of our existence.

Thursday 24

Friday 25

Saturday 26

Sunday 27

Pentecost (Whit Sunday)

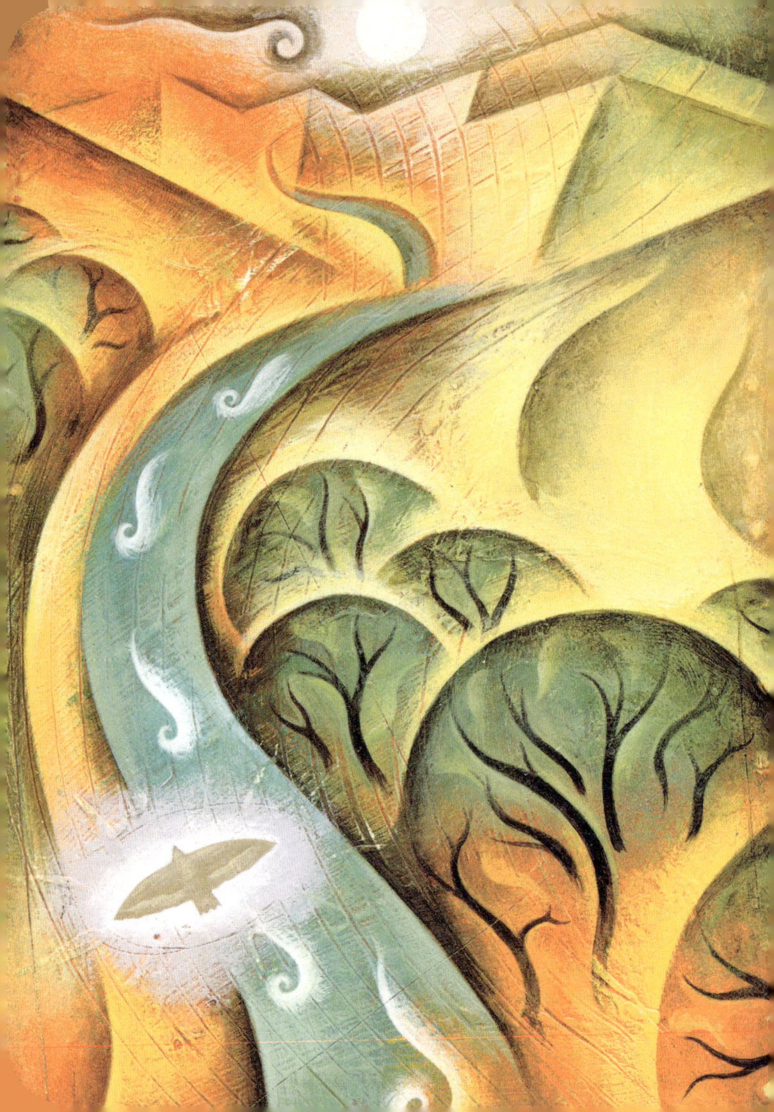

June

Connect with Nature

The natural world is our link to our deep animal self and the vast universe beyond. Indigenous peoples commune directly with the Earth and its creatures. Spending time outdoors allows us, too, to feel our kinship. Pick a totem animal and get to know it in the wild. Listen to birdsong in the forest. Serenade a sunset. It's time to learn nature's language and remember that we're all one under the stars.

Set Your Intention

I'm embracing my animal nature, and cultivating an intimate relationship with the Earth and its inhabitants. My guiding word is interconnection.

Practice: Praying with Your Body

The moon exerts a mystical pull on us, never more than when we meditate on it. Around the full moon (4 June), focus on channelling the heightened energy towards positive ends. The waning fourth-quarter moon (11 June) brings potential conflict; meditate on letting go. At the new moon (19 June), set goals and seed beginnings. With the waxing first-quarter moon (27 June), gather positive energy to pursue your goals.

Project: Pet Parenting

Pets are a portal back to nature. Watching Fido or Flora play is absorbing, but as a bonus it offers insight into human as well as animal behaviour. Just visit your local park: you'll see doggy bullies, doggy cliques and doggies in miniature sweaters. If you're not ready to share your life with a furry, feathered or slithery being, consider becoming a pet sitter or foster parent, or volunteering at an animal shelter.

May 28 - June 3

MAY
M	TU	W	TH	F	SA	SU
	1	2	3	4	5	6
7	8	9	10	11	12	13
14	15	16	17	18	19	20
21	22	23	24	25	26	27
28	29	30	31			

JUNE
M	TU	W	TH	F	SA	SU
				1	2	3
4	5	6	7	8	9	10
11	12	13	14	15	16	17
18	19	20	21	22	23	24
25	26	27	28	29	30	

JULY
M	TU	W	TH	F	SA	SU
						1
2	3	4	5	6	7	8
9	10	11	12	13	14	15
16	17	18	19	20	21	22
23	24	25	26	27	28	29
30	31					

Monday 28 ☾

Tuesday 29

Wednesday 30

---

*"Without inspiration the best powers of the mind remain dormant:
there is a fuel in us that needs to be ignited with sparks."*

JOHANN GOTTFRIED VAN HERDER (1744–1803)

The thinker's way

In Germany in the Romantic period, philosophers traditionally went on long walks in the countryside to ponder universal questions of faith and knowledge. In the midst of nature, the mind can breathe and be free of society's constraints. Go on a solo philosophy nature ramble and see if you can find the answer to some of life's conundrums. Then do the same walk again with a friend and debate your ideas.

Thursday 31

Friday 1

Saturday 2

Sunday 3

June 4 - June 10

MAY
M	TU	W	TH	F	SA	SU
	1	2	3	4	5	6
7	8	9	10	11	12	13
14	15	16	17	18	19	20
21	22	23	24	25	26	27
28	29	30	31			

JUNE
M	TU	W	TH	F	SA	SU
				1	2	3
4	5	6	7	8	9	10
11	12	13	14	15	16	17
18	19	20	21	22	23	24
25	26	27	28	29	30	

JULY
M	TU	W	TH	F	SA	SU
						1
2	3	4	5	6	7	8
9	10	11	12	13	14	15
16	17	18	19	20	21	22
23	24	25	26	27	28	29
30	31					

Monday 4
Spring Holiday (UK, Republic of Ireland)
Queen's Birthday celebrated (Holiday: New Zealand)

Tuesday 5
Queen's Diamond Jubilee (Holiday: UK)

Wednesday 6

"Great things are done when men and mountains meet.
This is not done by jostling in the street."

WILLIAM BLAKE (1757–1827)

Mountain high

The panorama offered by a mountaintop could be compared to heaven: you worked hard to get there and now you can unwind and enjoy it! Next time you trek up a mountain or a high hill, spend some time savouring not only the achievement of reaching the peak but also the exhilarating views. If the weather allows, stay up there for an hour or so. Revel in the fresh air and the thrilling perspectives.

Thursday 7

Friday 8

Saturday 9

Sunday 10

June 11 - June 17

MAY
M	TU	W	TH	F	SA	SU
	1	2	3	4	5	6
7	8	9	10	11	12	13
14	15	16	17	18	19	20
21	22	23	24	25	26	27
28	29	30	31			

JUNE
M	TU	W	TH	F	SA	SU
				1	2	3
4	5	6	7	8	9	10
11	**12**	**13**	**14**	**15**	**16**	**17**
18	19	20	21	22	23	24
25	26	27	28	29	30	

JULY
M	TU	W	TH	F	SA	SU
					1	
2	3	4	5	6	7	8
9	10	11	12	13	14	15
16	17	18	19	20	21	22
23	24	25	26	27	28	29
30	31					

Monday 11
Queen's Birthday celebrated (Holiday: Australia*, excluding Western Australia)

Tuesday 12

Wednesday 13

"A bird does not sing because it has an answer. It sings because it has a song."

CHINESE PROVERB

Air time

The fascination birds have for us is their mastery of an element that we may venture into from time to time but never fully inhabit. Add to this the amazing superlatives of the bird world – hummingbirds, for example, can fly backwards and flap their wings as fast as 90 times per second. Finally, if you need convincing, imagine a world without birdsong – how sterile our natural soundscape would become!

Thursday 14

Friday 15

Saturday 16

Sunday 17

Father's Day (UK)

June 18 - June 24

MAY						
M	TU	W	TH	F	SA	SU
	1	2	3	4	5	6
7	8	9	10	11	12	13
14	15	16	17	18	19	20
21	22	23	24	25	26	27
28	29	30	31			

JUNE						
M	TU	W	TH	F	SA	SU
				1	2	3
4	5	6	7	8	9	10
11	12	13	14	15	16	17
18	**19**	**20**	**21**	**22**	**23**	**24**
25	26	27	28	29	30	

JULY						
M	TU	W	TH	F	SA	SU
						1
2	3	4	5	6	7	8
9	10	11	12	13	14	15
16	17	18	19	20	21	22
23	24	25	26	27	28	29
30	31					

Monday 18

Tuesday 19

Wednesday 20

Summer Solstice

"The best remedy for those who are afraid, lonely, or unhappy is to go outside, somewhere they can be quiet, alone with the heavens, nature and God. Only then does one feel that all is as it should be."

ANNE FRANK (1929–1945)

Ancient stars

Awaken wonder by gazing at the constellations – through binoculars if you can. Follow the long "handle" of the Plough and you will reach the star Arcturus in the constellation Boötes, the Herdsman. The fourth brightest star, it is 36 lightyears from Earth. Drink in the majesty of this impossibly distant object. When modernity palls, take refreshment from the stars. Animated by ancient myth, they bear the lightest imprint of the imagination.

Thursday 21

Friday 22

Sun in Cancer

Saturday 23

Sunday 24

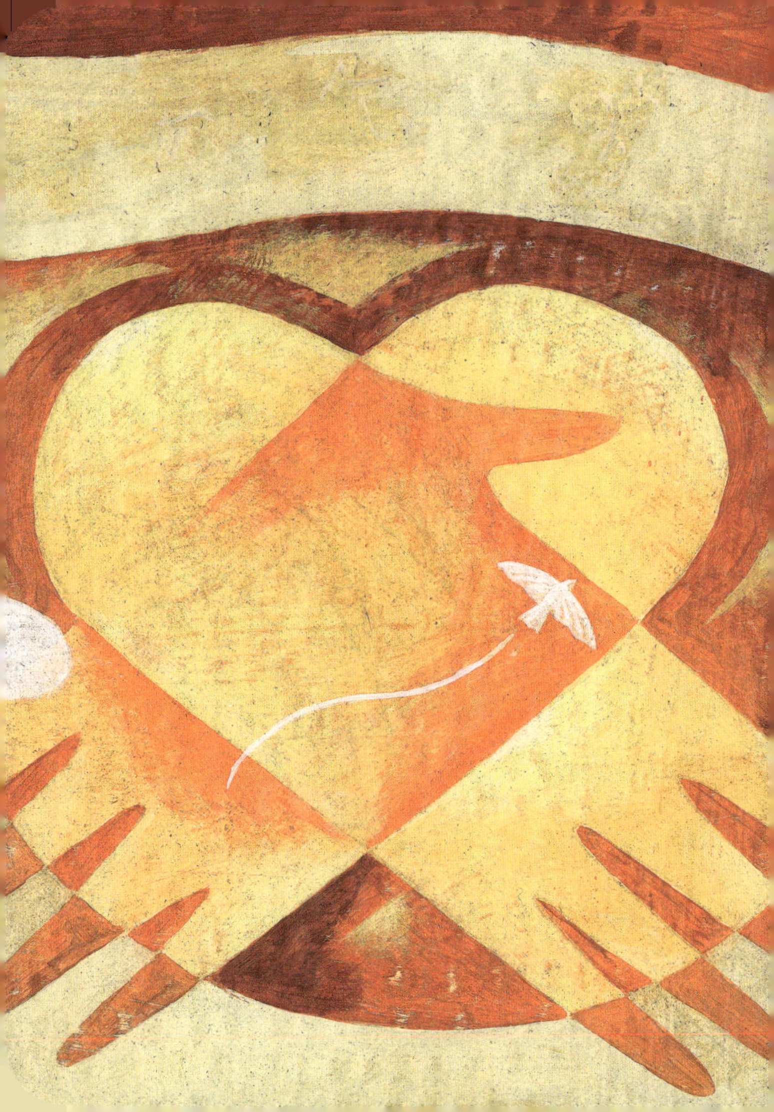

July

Cherish Others

We flourish in the presence of love and caring: no one grows and prospers alone. Nurture relationships with loved ones and foster a warm connection with everyone you meet. Those close to us are not only our best hedge against loneliness, they can be our biggest cheerleaders. "Never marry a person who is not a friend of your excitement," advises psychologist Nathaniel Brandon.

Set Your Intention

I'm cultivating caring relationships with family, friends and co-workers. I treat everyone I meet with warmth and respect. My guiding word is love.

Practice: Joy for Other People

When we see someone doing something kind or noble, we feel uplifted, inspired. Psychologist Jonathan Haidt calls this *elevation* – "rejoicing in virtue". Practise rejoicing not just in the good others do but in their good fortune as well. Start by sharing their delight in something easy to appreciate – a baby laughing, say – then move on to feeling pleased at their success. This practice opens your heart and transforms envy into love.

Project: Best Friends Forever

All of us are drawn to the idea of a kindred spirit with whom we are eternally bonded, sharing each other's secrets, offering balm for each other's hurts and laughing at jokes that only the two of us understand. Think of novel ways to honour your best friend. Design a mouse pad or pair of tennis shoes imprinted with her picture. Or create a calendar with photos of your (mis)adventures together: check out websites that walk you through the process.

June 25 - July 1

JUNE
M	TU	W	TH	F	SA	SU
					1	2	3
4	5	6	7	8	9	10
11	12	13	14	15	16	17
18	19	20	21	22	23	24
25	26	27	28	29	30	

JULY
M	TU	W	TH	F	SA	SU
						1
2	3	4	5	6	7	8
9	10	11	12	13	14	15
16	17	18	19	20	21	22
23	24	25	26	27	28	29
30	31					

AUGUST
M	TU	W	TH	F	SA	SU
	1	2	3	4	5	
6	7	8	9	10	11	12
13	14	15	16	17	18	19
20	21	22	23	24	25	26
27	28	29	30	31		

Monday 25

Tuesday 26

Wednesday 27 ☽

"Anyone who stops learning is old, whether at twenty or eighty. Anyone who keeps learning stays young. The greatest thing in life is to keep your mind young."

HENRY FORD (1863–1947)

Teacher's karma

To pass on wisdom or a skill is one of the noblest of all callings, and when we are benefiting someone close to us in this time-honoured way, the teacher's joys are doubled. From explaining to a child how to tie his or her shoelaces to training an elderly neighbour to surf the internet, teaching without thought of reward is a supreme example of selflessness, bringing good karma into our lives.

Thursday 28

Friday 29

Saturday 30

Sunday 1
Canada Day

July 2 - July 8

JUNE

M	TU	W	TH	F	SA	SU
				1	2	3
4	5	6	7	8	9	10
11	12	13	14	15	16	17
18	19	20	21	22	23	24
25	26	27	28	29	30	

JULY

M	TU	W	TH	F	SA	SU
2	3	4	5	6	7	8
9	10	11	12	13	14	15
16	17	18	19	20	21	22
23	24	25	26	27	28	29
30	31					

AUGUST

M	TU	W	TH	F	SA	SU
		1	2	3	4	5
6	7	8	9	10	11	12
13	14	15	16	17	18	19
20	21	22	23	24	25	26
27	28	29	30	31		

Monday 2

Tuesday 3

Wednesday 4
Independence Day (USA)

"There is one friend in the life of each of us who seems not a separate person, however dear and beloved, but an expansion, an interpretation, of one's self, the very meaning of one's soul."

EDITH WHARTON (1862–1937)

Special affinity

"Soulmates" is a word that is often applied to romantic partners – but in fact a soulmate can be someone with whom we share a special affinity that we think of as expressing a lifetime connection. Identify these invaluable people and make sure you don't drift apart from them. Modern technology makes communication quick and easy – even if there is no substitute for at least an annual get-together.

Thursday 5

Friday 6

Saturday 7

Sunday 8

July 9 - July 15

JUNE
M	TU	W	TH	F	SA	SU
				1	2	3
4	5	6	7	8	9	10
11	12	13	14	15	16	17
18	19	20	21	22	23	24
25	26	27	28	29	30	

JULY
M	TU	W	TH	F	SA	SU
					1	
2	3	4	5	6	7	8
9	**10**	**11**	**12**	**13**	**14**	**15**
16	17	18	19	20	21	22
23	24	25	26	27	28	29
30	31					

AUGUST
M	TU	W	TH	F	SA	SU
		1	2	3	4	5
6	7	8	9	10	11	12
13	14	15	16	17	18	19
20	21	22	23	24	25	26
27	28	29	30	31		

Monday 9

Tuesday 10

Wednesday 11 ☾

"Let your love be like the misty rains, coming softly, but flooding the river."
MALAGASY PROVERB

Crossing branches

To commit to a long-term relationship with someone is to entwine your life with theirs. You will always have your own memories, but even the experiences you have gathered while alone will connect with your partner's to create a complex dual history. Enjoy quiet times together, tracing your shared past and future in a spirit of loving celebration. Relish the complexity of your connections with each other and with the world beyond.

Thursday 12

Holiday (Northern Ireland)

Friday 13

Saturday 14

Bastille Day

Sunday 15

July 16 - July 22

JUNE

M	TU	W	TH	F	SA	SU
				1	2	3
4	5	6	7	8	9	10
11	12	13	14	15	16	17
18	19	20	21	22	23	24
25	26	27	28	29	30	

JULY

M	TU	W	TH	F	SA	SU
						1
2	3	4	5	6	7	8
9	10	11	12	13	14	15
16	**17**	**18**	**19**	**20**	**21**	**22**
23	24	25	26	27	28	29
30	31					

AUGUST

M	TU	W	TH	F	SA	SU
		1	2	3	4	5
6	7	8	9	10	11	12
13	14	15	16	17	18	19
20	21	22	23	24	25	26
27	28	29	30	31		

Monday 16

Tuesday 17

Wednesday 18

"Constant attention by a good nurse may be just as important as a major operation by a surgeon."

DAG HAMMARSKJÖLD (1905–1961)

Angel on duty

The nurturing instinct lies deep within all of us, and equips us well when loved ones or friends are sick. Release your inner Florence Nightingale – the famous nurse of the Crimean War. Do a first aid course. But above all, remember that what is most valued by the sick is warmth/coolness (depending on the climate), comfort and entertainment – store up stories, and don't expect to be entertained in return. This is pure giving.

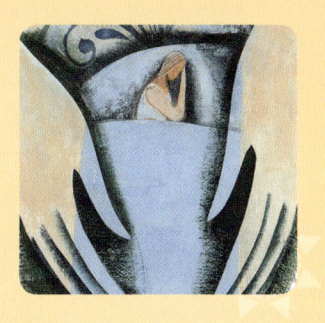

Thursday 19

Friday 20

Ramadan begins at sundown

Saturday 21

Sunday 22

July 23 - July 29

JUNE

M	TU	W	TH	F	SA	SU
				1	2	3
4	5	6	7	8	9	10
11	12	13	14	15	16	17
18	19	20	21	22	23	24
25	26	27	28	29	30	

JULY

M	TU	W	TH	F	SA	SU
						1
2	3	4	5	6	7	8
9	10	11	12	13	14	15
16	17	18	19	20	21	22
23	**24**	**25**	**26**	**27**	**28**	**29**
30	31					

AUGUST

M	TU	W	TH	F	SA	SU
		1	2	3	4	5
6	7	8	9	10	11	12
13	14	15	16	17	18	19
20	21	22	23	24	25	26
27	28	29	30	31		

Monday 23

Tuesday 24

Sun in Leo

Wednesday 25

"But if the while I think on thee, dear friend,
All losses are restored and sorrows end."
WILLIAM SHAKESPEARE (1564–1616), SONNET 30

The luck of the heart

Our greatest good fortune is the people we have the chance to meet, to learn from and to love. Think of your relationships as shells on a beach – there's an element of luck in them and an element of beauty. Treasure the accidents that brought you close to people you admire, respect and cherish. Those who doubt the power of destiny need look no further for proof of its benign operation in our lives.

Thursday 26

Friday 27

Saturday 28

Sunday 29

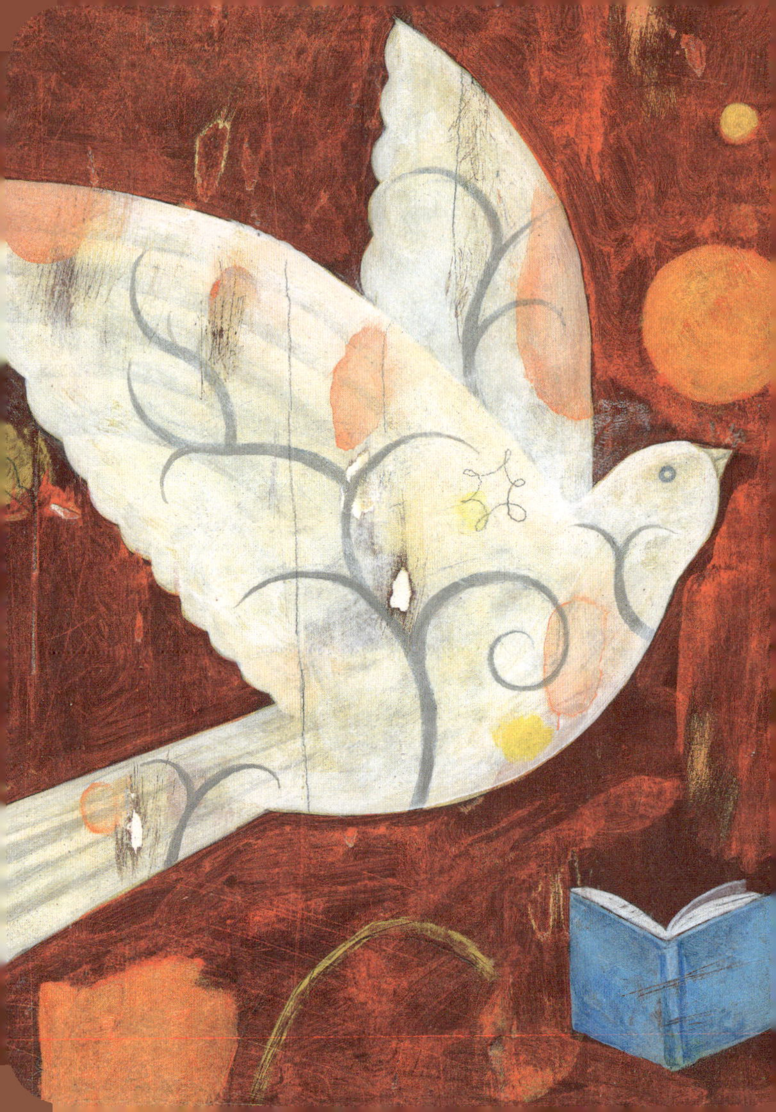

August

Cultivate Creativity

Imagination and originality fuel transformation. That kid we shunned as a geek grows up to change the world – think Steve Jobs and the iPod, iPhone and iPad or Mark Zuckerberg and Facebook. Then there's Leonardo da Vinci, the most creative polymath of all time. Great things are born out of curiosity, non-conformity, humour, divergent thinking. Cultivate your own creativity; find ways to help others develop theirs.

Set Your Intention

I'm open to new ideas springing from my own imagination and the fertile minds of others. I translate inspiration into concrete action. My guiding word is curiosity.

Practice: Zoning Out

A knitted brow and eye strain aren't the marks of a creative person. Look instead for a tinkerer, a trickster, a daydreamer. This month be that person: let your mind wander, play with ideas, mess around in your chosen medium, poke your nose into things. Read, visit museums, wander the streets, hang out with artists, listen to music – then lie back and do nothing. Let inspiration bubble up from your unconscious.

Project: Divine Inspiration

Assemble a creative pantheon to inspire you. Create an altar with pictures or talismanic objects to honour your gods and goddesses. You might include the Greek Muses; Saraswati, Hindu goddess of the arts; and Bragi, Norse god of creativity. Throw in a wild card: a wrathful Buddhist deity to destroy mental chatter and encourage focus, or a Native American *heyoka* like Coyote to turn your thinking inside out.

July 30 - August 5

JULY

M	TU	W	TH	F	SA	SU
						1
2	3	4	5	6	7	8
9	10	11	12	13	14	15
16	17	18	19	20	21	22
23	24	25	26	27	28	29
30	31					

AUGUST

M	TU	W	TH	F	SA	SU
	1	2	3	4	5	
6	7	8	9	10	11	12
13	14	15	16	17	18	19
20	21	22	23	24	25	26
27	28	29	30	31		

SEPTEMBER

M	TU	W	TH	F	SA	SU
					1	2
3	4	5	6	7	8	9
10	11	12	13	14	15	16
17	18	19	20	21	22	23
24	25	26	27	28	29	30

Monday 30

Tuesday 31

Wednesday 1
Lughnasadh (Lammas)

*"The most beautiful thing we can experience is the mysterious.
It is the source of all true art and science."*

ALBERT EINSTEIN (1879–1955)

Moonstone talisman

In India and Sri Lanka, moonstone is the Ayurvedic stone for women, embodying Goddess energy and lunar power. Keep one with you as a talisman on your desk or worktop to release your innate creativity. Hold it in your hand – if there's a full moon, take the stone outside and lift it in your outstretched palm to soak up the moon's radiance. It's a creative battery: you have only to touch it and your imagination should feel a subtle change.

Thursday 2

Friday 3

Saturday 4

Sunday 5

August 6 - August 12

JULY

M	TU	W	TH	F	SA	SU
						1
2	3	4	5	6	7	8
9	10	11	12	13	14	15
16	17	18	19	20	21	22
23	24	25	26	27	28	29
30	31					

AUGUST

M	TU	W	TH	F	SA	SU
		1	2	3	4	5
6	7	8	9	10	11	12
13	14	15	16	17	18	19
20	21	22	23	24	25	26
27	28	29	30	31		

SEPTEMBER

M	TU	W	TH	F	SA	SU
					1	2
3	4	5	6	7	8	9
10	11	12	13	14	15	16
17	18	19	20	21	22	23
24	25	26	27	28	29	30

Monday 6
August Holiday
(Scotland, Republic of Ireland)

Tuesday 7

Wednesday 8

"I never travel without my diary. One should always have something sensational to read in the train."

OSCAR WILDE (1854–1900)

Stillness on the move

The enforced stillness of a journey on public transport, such as a train or an aeroplane, provided that it's a comfortable one, can encourage creative thinking. Ideally, you need a couple of hours. Use the time to write a manifesto – even just keywords, like "surprise", "penetration" or "connections" to help focus your ideas. Sketch out a project that would encompass the principles you have stated.

Thursday 9

Friday 10

Saturday 11

Sunday 12

August 13 - August 19

JULY

M	TU	W	TH	F	SA	SU
						1
2	3	4	5	6	7	8
9	10	11	12	13	14	15
16	17	18	19	20	21	22
23	24	25	26	27	28	29
30	31					

AUGUST

M	TU	W	TH	F	SA	SU
	1	2	3	4	5	
6	7	8	9	10	11	12
13	14	15	16	17	18	19
20	21	22	23	24	25	26
27	28	29	30	31		

SEPTEMBER

M	TU	W	TH	F	SA	SU
				1	2	
3	4	5	6	7	8	9
10	11	12	13	14	15	16
17	18	19	20	21	22	23
24	25	26	27	28	29	30

Monday 13

Tuesday 14

Wednesday 15

"It is sweet to let the mind unbend on occasion."
HORACE (65–8 BCE)

Monkey magic

Buddhists speak disparagingly of the "monkey mind", always flitting about from one place to another, but there are qualities in the monkey that can benefit creativity – nimbleness, combined with an element (sometimes) of mischief. The creative person cannot afford to be a conformist. The more you challenge habit, cliché and formula, the greater the rewards to your sense of the creative self.

Thursday 16

Friday 17

Saturday 18

Sunday 19
Ramadan ends

August 20 - August 26

JULY
M	TU	W	TH	F	SA	SU
						1
2	3	4	5	6	7	8
9	10	11	12	13	14	15
16	17	18	19	20	21	22
23	24	25	26	27	28	29
30	31					

AUGUST
M	TU	W	TH	F	SA	SU
		1	2	3	4	5
6	7	8	9	10	11	12
13	14	15	16	17	18	19
20	**21**	**22**	**23**	**24**	**25**	**26**
27	28	29	30	31		

SEPTEMBER
M	TU	W	TH	F	SA	SU
					1	2
3	4	5	6	7	8	9
10	11	12	13	14	15	16
17	18	19	20	21	22	23
24	25	26	27	28	29	30

Monday 20

Tuesday 21

Wednesday 22

"All great deeds and all great thoughts have a ridiculous beginning."
ALBERT CAMUS (1913–1960)

Looking sideways

Unexpected angles produce striking results: let this be the mantra of your imagination. You can read this message in various ways. For example, taking a sidelong look could mean catching people unawares when taking a photograph. Or it might mean looking at what's going on in the cake-decorator's mind if you are writing a story about a wedding. In fact, the principle applies to life in general: look differently and you'll see things afresh.

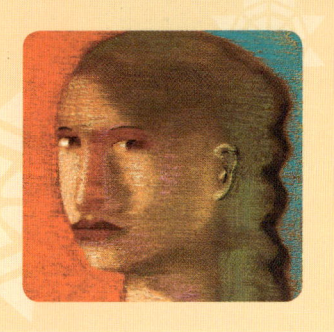

Thursday 23

Friday 24 ☽

Sun in Virgo

Saturday 25

Sunday 26

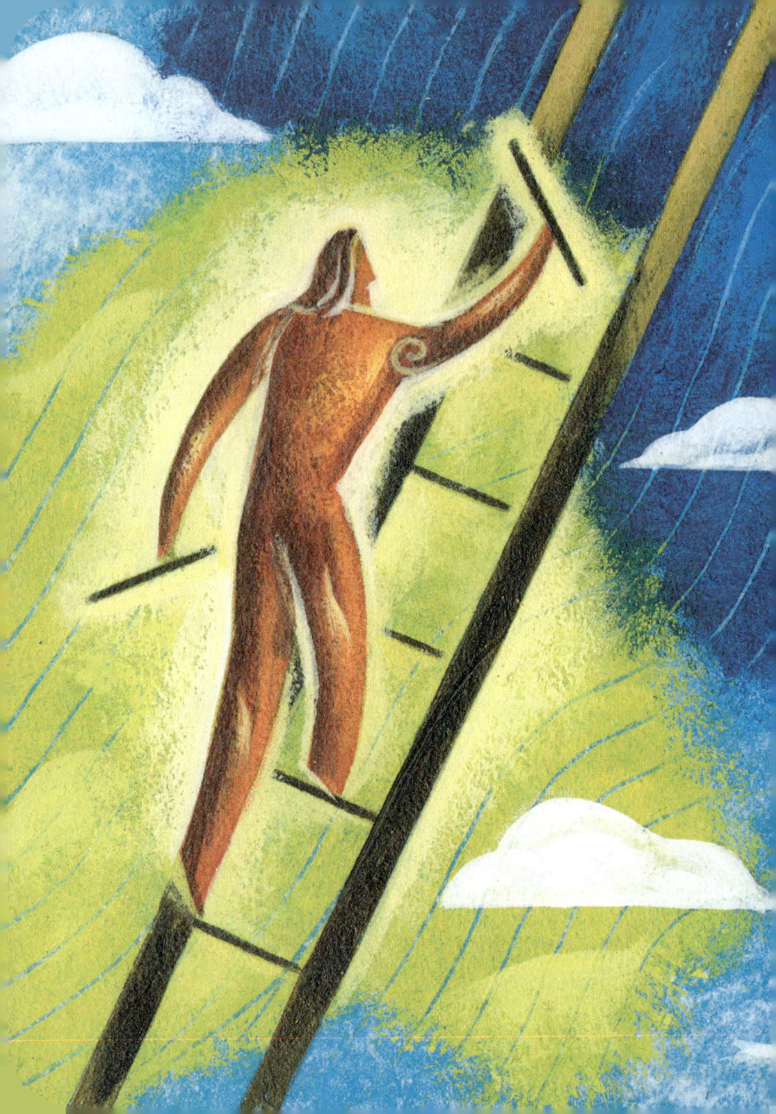

September

Achieve Mastery

Become really, really good at something: even if it's just learning to change a tyre, experience the thrill of mastery. See how achievement broadens your perspective, encouraging you to learn even more (replacing the spark plugs?). Developing skill or knowledge teaches us patience and perseverance. Raw talent is nothing without drive and dedication. Sometimes all that keeps us from succeeding is laziness.

Set Your Intention

I'm developing my skill and expertise in my chosen area. I'm dedicated to mastering it. My guiding word is perseverance.

Practice: Starting Again

Anyone learning a musical instrument knows that you start playing, make a mistake, then start again. And again. That's pretty much how mastering anything is. Even experts know that it's only with practice and persistence that they can finally nail it. Whatever you're trying to achieve, practise beginning again until you succeed. Do it again and again: the path to mastery will slowly unfold before you.

Project: Crazy Wisdom

Intuition, some say, is the key to handling information overload. When digesting a barrage of input, just sit with it. Wait for a gut response. Out-of-left-field, I-don't-know-how-I-know-it-but-I-do knowledge that defies reason is almost always spot on. Invite it, trust it, don't dismiss its zany logic. Intuition is mastery's silent partner.

August 27 - September 2

AUGUST
M	TU	W	TH	F	SA	SU
	1	2	3	4	5	
6	7	8	9	10	11	12
13	14	15	16	17	18	19
20	21	22	23	24	25	26
27	28	29	30	31		

SEPTEMBER
M	TU	W	TH	F	SA	SU
					1	2
3	4	5	6	7	8	9
10	11	12	13	14	15	16
17	18	19	20	21	22	23
24	25	26	27	28	29	30

OCTOBER
M	TU	W	TH	F	SA	SU
1	2	3	4	5	6	7
8	9	10	11	12	13	14
15	16	17	18	19	20	21
22	23	24	25	26	27	28
29	30	31				

Monday 27
Late Summer Holiday
(UK, excluding Scotland)

Tuesday 28

Wednesday 29

"For thou hast made him a little lower than the angels, and has crowned him with glory and with honour."

PSALMS 8:5

Mind and muscle

The Centaur in Greek myth – half man and half horse – is often seen as a symbol of animal instincts, but it can also be interpreted more positively. Chiron, the most famous Centaur, showed strength and ability in the service of right. To apply mind and body equally in a task, as (for example) a marathon runner does, has special value. Look for opportunities for mind and muscle to work together – ideally, for the sake of others.

Thursday 30

Friday 31

Saturday 1

Sunday 2

Father's Day (Australia, New Zealand)

September 3 - September 9

AUGUST

M	TU	W	TH	F	SA	SU
		1	2	3	4	5
6	7	8	9	10	11	12
13	14	15	16	17	18	19
20	21	22	23	24	25	26
27	28	29	30	31		

SEPTEMBER

M	TU	W	TH	F	SA	SU
					1	2
3	4	5	6	7	8	9
10	11	12	13	14	15	16
17	18	19	20	21	22	23
24	25	26	27	28	29	30

OCTOBER

M	TU	W	TH	F	SA	SU
1	2	3	4	5	6	7
8	9	10	11	12	13	14
15	16	17	18	19	20	21
22	23	24	25	26	27	28
29	30	31				

Monday 3

Tuesday 4

Wednesday 5

"Most of us serve our ideals by fits and starts. The person who makes a success of living is one who sees his goal steadily and aims for it unswervingly. That's dedication."

CECIL B. DEMILLE (1881–1959)

Toward a distant goal

When far-off goals seem unattainable, lay out a realistic path toward them and take the journey one step at a time. Keep the distant goal in view, and measure your progress not by how close it seems but by the quality of the steps you are taking. Are they hopeful and resolved, or tentative and anxious? It's fine to retrace your steps when you need to – but when you are going forward, do so with purpose and hope.

Thursday 6

Friday 7

Saturday 8

Sunday 9

September 10 - September 16

AUGUST

M	TU	W	TH	F	SA	SU
		1	2	3	4	5
6	7	8	9	10	11	12
13	14	15	16	17	18	19
20	21	22	23	24	25	26
27	28	29	30	31		

SEPTEMBER

M	TU	W	TH	F	SA	SU
					1	2
3	4	5	6	7	8	9
10	**11**	**12**	**13**	**14**	**15**	**16**
17	18	19	20	21	22	23
24	25	26	27	28	29	30

OCTOBER

M	TU	W	TH	F	SA	SU
1	2	3	4	5	6	7
8	9	10	11	12	13	14
15	16	17	18	19	20	21
22	23	24	25	26	27	28
29	30	31				

Monday 10

Tuesday 11

Wednesday 12

"Talking is like playing on the harp; there is as much in laying the hands on the strings to stop their vibration as in twanging them to bring out their music."

OLIVER WENDELL HOLMES (1809–1894)

Speaking well

Our language is more than a means of communicating with others: at its best it is a celebration of the astonishing power of the human brain and of the triumph of mind over matter. Aspire to eloquence: all it takes is speaking thoughtfully, allowing your intelligence and your imagination to choose your words and shape your sentences. Relish the spoken word: by doing so you will give pleasure to your listeners and to yourself.

Thursday 13

Friday 14

Saturday 15

Sunday 16

Rosh Hashanah (Jewish New Year) begins at sundown

September 17 - September 23

AUGUST

M	TU	W	TH	F	SA	SU
	1	2	3	4	5	6
6	7	8	9	10	11	12
13	14	15	16	17	18	19
20	21	22	23	24	25	26
27	28	29	30	31		

SEPTEMBER

M	TU	W	TH	F	SA	SU
					1	2
3	4	5	6	7	8	9
10	11	12	13	14	15	16
17	**18**	**19**	**20**	**21**	**22**	**23**
24	25	26	27	28	29	30

OCTOBER

M	TU	W	TH	F	SA	SU
1	2	3	4	5	6	7
8	9	10	11	12	13	14
15	16	17	18	19	20	21
22	23	24	25	26	27	28
29	30	31				

Monday 17

Tuesday 18

Wednesday 19

"Fool me once, shame on you; fool me twice, shame on me."
CHINESE PROVERB

Fruits of experience

We learn from our achievements and our mistakes, but it's easy to let both slip into oblivion – especially our mistakes, which it is all too tempting to bury in the drifting sands of the unconscious. Harvest your efforts with care, setting aside both successes and failures for further study. Hold mistakes up in the clear light of day without embarrassment. Not all are avoidable – learn from the ones that were and the ones that were not.

Thursday 20

Friday 21
Peace Day

Saturday 22
Autumn Equinox

Sunday 23

September 24 – September 30

AUGUST
M	TU	W	TH	F	SA	SU
	1	2	3	4	5	
6	7	8	9	10	11	12
13	14	15	16	17	18	19
20	21	22	23	24	25	26
27	28	29	30	31		

SEPTEMBER
M	TU	W	TH	F	SA	SU
				1	2	3
4	5	6	7	8	9	10
11	12	13	14	15	16	17
18	19	20	21	22	23	
24	**25**	**26**	**27**	**28**	**29**	**30**

OCTOBER
M	TU	W	TH	F	SA	SU
1	2	3	4	5	6	7
8	9	10	11	12	13	14
15	16	17	18	19	20	21
22	23	24	25	26	27	28
29	30	31				

Monday 24
Sun in Libra

Tuesday 25
Yom Kippur (Day of Atonement) begins at sundown

Wednesday 26

"A book reads the better which is our own, and has been so long known to us, that we know the topography of its blots, and dog's ears, and can trace the dirt in it to having read it at tea with buttered muffins."

CHARLES LAMB (1775–1834)

Expert witness

There is virtually no human endeavour on which expert practitioners have been reticent. Whatever skill or subject you are attempting to master, you will find truckloads of advice on the internet, but it's more satisfying to buy a second-hand book on the subject – second-hand, because you can then feel free to write in the margins. Use this blank space to affirm your commitment to learn from the master and attain your own levels of excellence.

Thursday 27

Friday 28

Saturday 29

Sunday 30

Hudson Bay
Gulf of Mexico
Caribbean Sea
Sea
Atlas Mountains
Sahara

October

Join Forces

Now and then something happens – a signal event, a catastrophe even – that wakes us up to how interconnected we are and how much we need to pull together. Your challenge now is to apply that knowledge. As your perspective expands, bring that increased awareness to a larger arena. Make a localized investment of your concern for all beings. Speak out, be a force for good, collaborate. Think "we" instead of "me".

Set Your Intention

I'm offering the fruits of my inner growth to the world. I help wherever my expertise is needed. My guiding word is cooperation.

Practice: Say "We"

A woman who was close to Mother Teresa recalls that in conversation and correspondence, Mother never began a sentence with "I". Talk about humility! Practise putting "I" in its place. It may take some creative rephrasing, but that will make you more aware of what you say and how you say it, in speaking or in writing. While you're at it, practise using "we" instead of "I" when referring to any group effort.

Project: Working Partners

Alone I can do my small part, but together we can move the Earth – provided we pick the right partners. Research shows that the people we hang out with can reinforce our worst habits. But the converse is also true: consider Twelve Step programs, where peer support helps people stay away from their addictions. You don't have to be best chums to collaborate effectively. Just focus on your common goal.

October 1 - October 7

SEPTEMBER

M	TU	W	TH	F	SA	SU
					1	2
3	4	5	6	7	8	9
10	11	12	13	14	15	16
17	18	19	20	21	22	23
24	25	26	27	28	29	30

OCTOBER

M	TU	W	TH	F	SA	SU
1	2	3	4	5	6	7
8	9	10	11	12	13	14
15	16	17	18	19	20	21
22	23	24	25	26	27	28
29	30	31				

NOVEMBER

M	TU	W	TH	F	SA	SU
			1	2	3	4
5	6	7	8	9	10	11
12	13	14	15	16	17	18
19	20	21	22	23	24	25
26	27	28	29	30	31	

Monday 1

Queen's Birthday celebrated: Holiday (Western Australia*), Labour Day (Australian Capital Territory, NSW, South Australia)

Tuesday 2

Wednesday 3

"The better friends you are, the straighter you can talk, but while you are only on nodding terms, be slow to scold."

ST. FRANCIS XAVIER (1506–1552)

Café club

Create your own community hub within a suitable local café or juice bar. Cultivate the friendship of the owners and win their support for establishing the place as a neighbourhood centre. Start with a noticeboard, then progress to a local network meeting – morning, lunchtime or evening. See if you can raise the funds for a café website. Improvise from there to build up your local awareness and activity group.

Thursday 4

Friday 5

Saturday 6

Sunday 7

October 8 - October 14

SEPTEMBER

M	TU	W	TH	F	SA	SU
					1	2
3	4	5	6	7	8	9
10	11	12	13	14	15	16
17	18	19	20	21	22	23
24	25	26	27	28	29	30

OCTOBER

M	TU	W	TH	F	SA	SU
1	2	3	4	5	6	7
8	9	10	11	12	13	14
15	16	17	18	19	20	21
22	23	24	25	26	27	28
29	30	31				

NOVEMBER

M	TU	W	TH	F	SA	SU
			1	2	3	4
5	6	7	8	9	10	11
12	13	14	15	16	17	18
19	20	21	22	23	24	25
26	27	28	29	30		

Monday 8

Thanksgiving Day (Canada)

Tuesday 9

Wednesday 10

"My piece of bread only belongs to me when I know that everyone else has a share, and that no one starves whilst I eat."

LEO TOLSTOY (1828–1919)

Shadow shopping

Ask around your neighbourhood to establish if there's anyone living nearby who finds it difficult to get out of the house to do their weekly shopping – maybe a single parent or someone who is elderly. Let them know when your shopping trips are scheduled and how to contact you to place their order. Afterwards, they could either pick up from you or, better still, you could deliver to them. What better way to show social compassion?

Thursday 11

Friday 12

Saturday 13

Sunday 14

October 15 - October 21

SEPTEMBER

M	TU	W	TH	F	SA	SU
					1	2
3	4	5	6	7	8	9
10	11	12	13	14	15	16
17	18	19	20	21	22	23
24	25	26	27	28	29	30

OCTOBER

M	TU	W	TH	F	SA	SU
1	2	3	4	5	6	7
8	9	10	11	12	13	14
15	**16**	**17**	**18**	**19**	**20**	**21**
22	23	24	25	26	27	28
29	30	31				

NOVEMBER

M	TU	W	TH	F	SA	SU
			1	2	3	4
5	6	7	8	9	10	11
12	13	14	15	16	17	18
19	20	21	22	23	24	25
26	27	28	29	30	31	

Monday 15 ○

Tuesday 16

Wednesday 17

"Perhaps you can acquire wisdom simply by taking a gentle stroll around your village with a friend or two to help you notice things."

HENRIK IBSEN (1828–1906)

Local tour

Every neighbourhood has its secret stories to tell: the buildings may be unremarkable, but the lives of the people who have lived and worked there are likely to contain hidden gems of fascinating fact. There might even be connections with regional or national history. Form a research group with friends who are interested in local history. Take visitors on a tour of key landmarks and share with them the stories you unearth.

Thursday 18

Friday 19

Saturday 20

Sunday 21

October 22 - October 28

SEPTEMBER

M	TU	W	TH	F	SA	SU
					1	2
3	4	5	6	7	8	9
10	11	12	13	14	15	16
17	18	19	20	21	22	23
24	25	26	27	28	29	30

OCTOBER

M	TU	W	TH	F	SA	SU
1	2	3	4	5	6	7
8	9	10	11	12	13	14
15	16	17	18	19	20	21
22	23	24	25	26	27	28
29	30	31				

NOVEMBER

M	TU	W	TH	F	SA	SU
			1	2	3	4
5	6	7	8	9	10	11
12	13	14	15	16	17	18
19	20	21	22	23	24	25
26	27	28	29	30		

Monday 22 ☾

Labour Day (New Zealand)

Tuesday 23

Wednesday 24

Sun in Scorpio

"I expect to pass through life but once. If therefore, there be any kindness I can show, or any good thing I can do to any fellow being, let me do it now, and not defer or neglect it, as I shall not pass this way again."

WILLIAM PENN (1644–1718)

Many hands

Nobody has more than one pair of hands, and some chores seem to take forever. Form an Octopus club with up to a half-dozen friends – a loose cooperative arrangement whereby everyone benefits from those extra pairs of hands. Write a constitution for the group, and as many rules as you want to think up. You could use a voucher system to keep track of favours done and ensure that the work evens out over time.

Thursday 25

Friday 26

Saturday 27

Sunday 28
British Summer Time ends

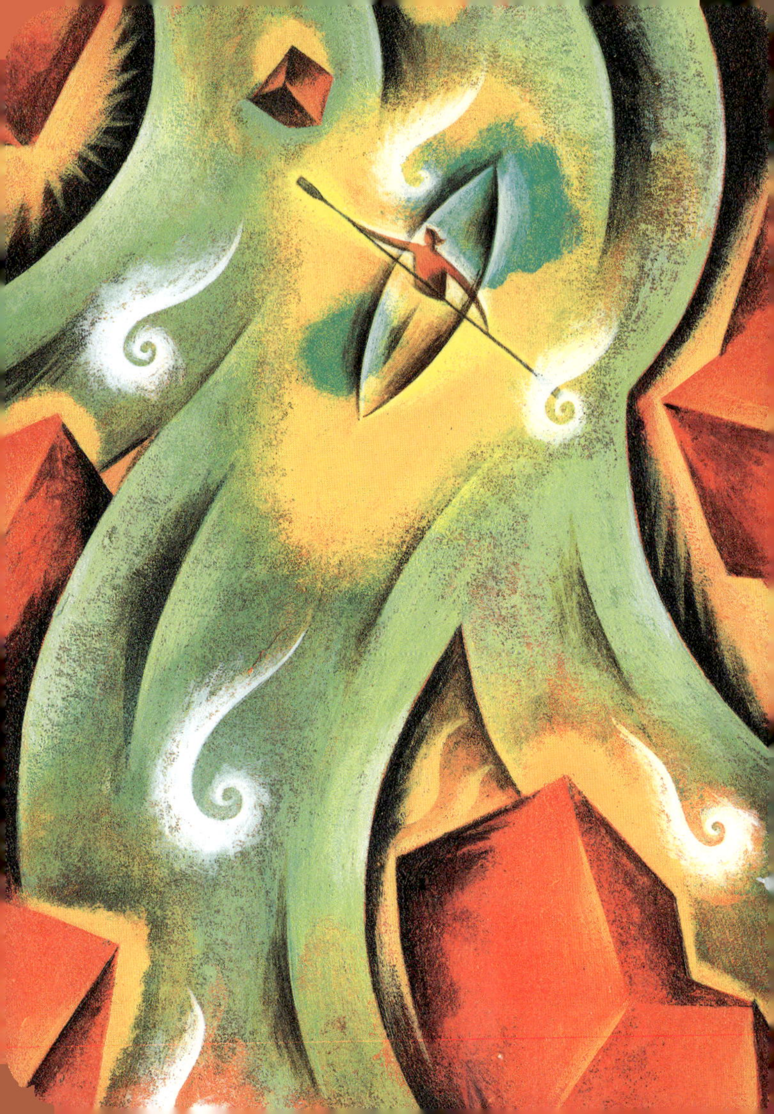

November

Be Bold

OK, so you weren't the kid who dared everyone to swim across the canal or ring the eccentric neighbour's doorbell. But now you have everything to gain from showing a little pluck. No need to be foolhardy. Just take on something you swore you couldn't or wouldn't do, and see how far you can go with it. Run with the wolves; shake up the status quo. You won't know your strength until you test yourself.

Set Your Intention

I'm ready to take risks to accomplish meaningful goals. I have what it takes to step into the unknown. My guiding word is courage.

Practice: Flying Blind

We're so used to relying on technology to guide us that we forget we have a built-in positioning system in the brain to help us stay on course. Next time you're lost – or going somewhere unfamiliar – before you phone for help or check your GPS, see if you can find your way by instinct, observation and logic. (Did you notice where the sun was at that last turn, for example?) Trust your resourcefulness.

Project: Run for Office

Tired of the way things are being managed at your company or housing association or community group? Put yourself on the line. Lobby for the job of being in charge. Mount a campaign. Back it up with facts. Have a plan for how to do the job better or more profitably. Gather supporters. Even if it's only organizing the carpool or arranging the flowers at church, dare to be a catalyst for change.

October 29 - November 4

OCTOBER

M	TU	W	TH	F	SA	SU
1	2	3	4	5	6	7
8	9	10	11	12	13	14
15	16	17	18	19	20	21
22	23	24	25	26	27	28
29	30	31				

NOVEMBER

M	TU	W	TH	F	SA	SU
			1	2	3	4
5	6	7	8	9	10	11
12	13	14	15	16	17	18
19	20	21	22	23	24	25
26	27	28	29	30	31	

DECEMBER

M	TU	W	TH	F	SA	SU
					1	2
3	4	5	6	7	8	9
10	11	12	13	14	15	16
17	18	19	20	21	22	23
24	25	26	27	28	29	30
31						

Monday 29
October Holiday
(Republic of Ireland)

Tuesday 30

Wednesday 31
Halloween
Samhain

"Don't stand by the water longing for fish: go home and weave a net."
CHINESE PROVERB

The arc of action

Procrastination can come from many sources, including fear of failure, fear of success, negative self-belief, being too busy, being disorganized or simply poor time management. The cost of dithering is often a build-up of anxiety, starting off a cycle of stress. Reflect on this and resolve to rid yourself of anxiety by taking action. Follow this three-step strategy: plan, resolve, plunge. Be prepared to change your plan in the light of the unexpected.

Thursday 1

All Saints' Day

Friday 2

All Souls' Day

Saturday 3

Sunday 4

November 5 - November 11

OCTOBER

M	TU	W	TH	F	SA	SU
1	2	3	4	5	6	7
8	9	10	11	12	13	14
15	16	17	18	19	20	21
22	23	24	25	26	27	28
29	30	31				

NOVEMBER

M	TU	W	TH	F	SA	SU
			1	2	3	4
5	6	7	8	9	10	11
12	13	14	15	16	17	18
19	20	21	22	23	24	25
26	27	28	29	30	31	

DECEMBER

M	TU	W	TH	F	SA	SU
					1	2
3	4	5	6	7	8	9
10	11	12	13	14	15	16
17	18	19	20	21	22	23
24	25	26	27	28	29	30
31						

Monday 5

Tuesday 6

Wednesday 7

"Man is most nearly himself when he achieves the seriousness of a child at play."
HERACLITUS (c.535– c.475 BCE)

Pantomime

Performing comedy in front of an audience of children is a noble sacrifice of an adult's time. Kids respond well to warmth, humour and effort, and won't mark you down on technicalities. You may feel fear beforehand – but that's precisely why should give it a try. Entertaining children in public – with a glove puppet or conjurer's tricks or knockabout humour à la Buster Keaton – purges the ego of its pretensions. You may even have lots of fun!

Thursday 8

Friday 9

Saturday 10

Sunday 11

November 12 - November 18

OCTOBER

M	TU	W	TH	F	SA	SU
1	2	3	4	5	6	7
8	9	10	11	12	13	14
15	16	17	18	19	20	21
22	23	24	25	26	27	28
29	30	31				

NOVEMBER

M	TU	W	TH	F	SA	SU
			1	2	3	4
5	6	7	8	9	10	11
12	**13**	**14**	**15**	**16**	**17**	**18**
19	20	21	22	23	24	25
26	27	28	29	30		

DECEMBER

M	TU	W	TH	F	SA	SU
					1	2
3	4	5	6	7	8	9
10	11	12	13	14	15	16
17	18	19	20	21	22	23
24	25	26	27	28	29	30
31						

Monday 12

Tuesday 13 ●

Diwali
Remembrance Day

Wednesday 14

"The greatest enemy of any one of our truths may be the rest of our truths."
WILLIAM JAMES (1842–1910)

Crystal dowsing

Dowsing offers evidence that humankind has faculties beyond the understanding of science. You can dowse for water or for lost objects or to find the answer to a question or resolve a dilemma. Buy a crystal pendulum, then get a friend to bury a coin or hide it under a large rug. Hang the pendulum from one hand and walk slowly around the area. If you relax and dismiss any scepticism, the pendulum should swing when it's above the coin.

Thursday 15

Islamic New Year (Muharram)

Friday 16

Saturday 17

Sunday 18

November 19 - November 25

OCTOBER

M	TU	W	TH	F	SA	SU
1	2	3	4	5	6	7
8	9	10	11	12	13	14
15	16	17	18	19	20	21
22	23	24	25	26	27	28
29	30	31				

NOVEMBER

M	TU	W	TH	F	SA	SU
			1	2	3	4
5	6	7	8	9	10	11
12	13	14	15	16	17	18
19	20	21	22	23	24	25
26	27	28	29	30		

DECEMBER

M	TU	W	TH	F	SA	SU
					1	2
3	4	5	6	7	8	9
10	11	12	13	14	15	16
17	18	19	20	21	22	23
24	25	26	27	28	29	30
31						

Monday 19

Tuesday 20

Wednesday 21

World Hello Day

"Opportunites fly by while we sit regretting the chances we have lost, and the happiness that comes to us we heed not, because of the happiness that is gone."

JEROME K. JEROME (1859–1927)

Stretch yourself

There is dignity in physical labour, though many of us may be daunted by the prospect of exerting neglected muscles. The secret is knowing your limits and staying well within them. A small project such as building a wall, creating a garden pond or rockery or hanging a gate can be immensely satisfying – especially if you have to read up on new skills beforehand. Dare to stretch yourself – in all senses of the word.

Thursday 22
Thanksgiving Day (USA)

Friday 23
Sun in Sagittarius

Saturday 24

Sunday 25

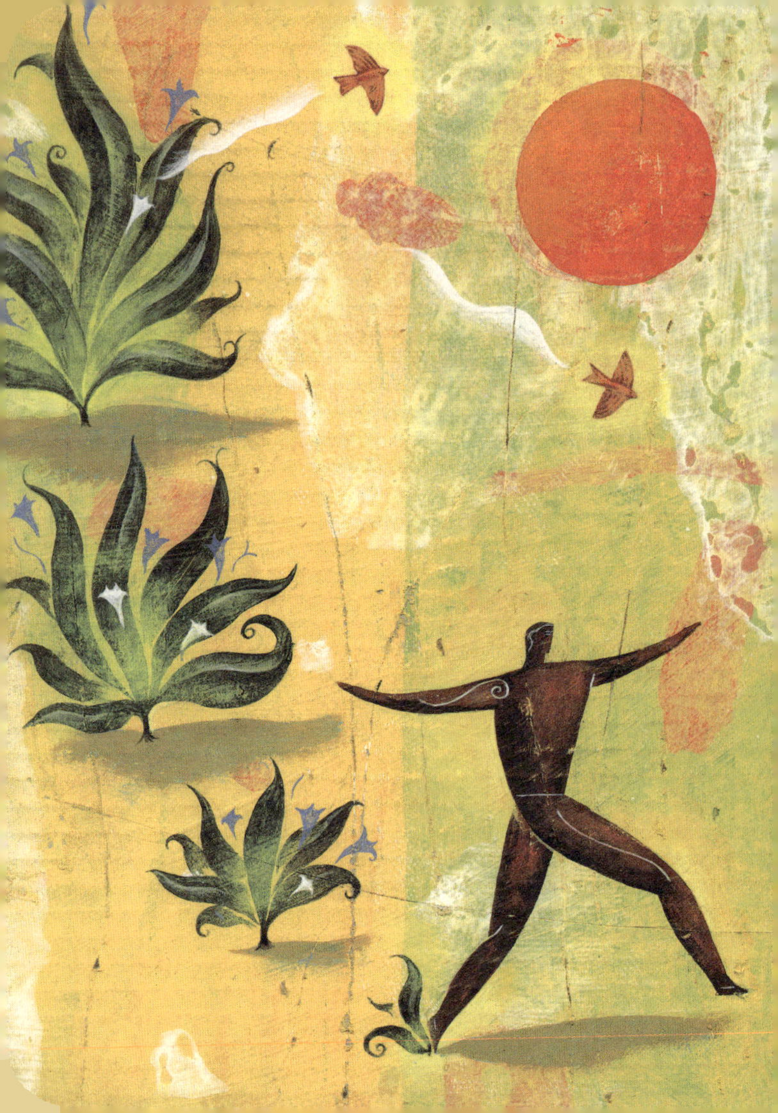

December

Celebrate Transformation

You did it! It's December and you're a different person. Yes, you're still recognizable as you. But you've made significant changes in your life and taken steps to improve conditions around you. Congratulations are in order. As you celebrate what you've achieved, remember, the journey of transformation isn't a solo excursion. Be sure to thank all who've walked alongside you or supported your efforts.

Set Your Intention

I'm living the change I set out to make this year. I'm bringing peace and joy to the world. My guiding word is expansion.

Practice: Embracing Change

Light a candle and reflect on the ways you've changed. Really take in the extent of the transformation. Review where you were at the start of the year, then recall turning points in the months since. Think of the people you collaborated with or who gave you a hand. Note anything unfinished that you want to complete next year. Before you blow out the candle, ask Spirit for the power to continue your good work.

Project: End-Time Celebration

Mayanist experts say that if the ancient Maya were around, they'd probably throw a party for the end of their calendar. So why not hold your own celebration on Solstice eve, 20 December? Incorporate aspects of all the seasonal holidays; toss the yule log on the fire. And dream up your own rituals for this once-in-5,125-years occasion. Invite everyone you know, in case the world really does end on 21 December.

November 26 - December 2

NOVEMBER

SU	M	TU	W	TH	F	SA
			1	2	3	4
5	6	7	8	9	10	11
12	13	14	15	16	17	18
19	20	21	22	23	24	25
26	27	28	29	30		

DECEMBER

SU	M	TU	W	TH	F	SA
					1	2
3	4	5	6	7	8	9
10	11	12	13	14	15	16
17	18	19	20	21	22	23
24	25	26	27	28	29	30
31						

JANUARY

SU	M	TU	W	TH	F	SA
	1	2	3	4	5	6
7	8	9	10	11	12	13
14	15	16	17	18	19	20
21	22	23	24	25	26	27
28	29	30	31			

Monday 26

Tuesday 27

Wednesday 28 ●

"Not being able to govern events, I govern myself, and apply myself to them, if they will not apply themselves to me."

MICHEL DE MONTAIGNE (1533–1592)

Salamander spirit

The salamander, a lizard-like creature believed by the ancients to be born in fire, is a powerful symbol of inner transformation and of the self-discipline needed to resist temptation. Imagine its body within your body, its limbs within your limbs. Feel the cold dowsing power of the salamander taking the heat out of your material self, halting the appetites in their tracks. Witness the upsurge of spirit – a deep sense of harmony and grace.

Thursday 29

Friday 30

St Andrew's Day (Holiday: Scotland)

Saturday 1

Sunday 2
First Sunday in Advent

December 3 - December 9

NOVEMBER

M	TU	W	TH	F	SA	SU
				1	2	3
4	5	6	7	8	9	10
11	12	13	14	15	16	17
18	19	20	21	22	23	24
25	26	27	28	29	30	

DECEMBER

M	TU	W	TH	F	SA	SU
					1	2
3	**4**	**5**	**6**	**7**	**8**	**9**
10	11	12	13	14	15	16
17	18	19	20	21	22	23
24	25	26	27	28	29	30
31						

JANUARY

M	TU	W	TH	F	SA	SU
	1	2	3	4	5	6
7	8	9	10	11	12	13
14	15	16	17	18	19	20
21	22	23	24	25	26	27
28	29	30	31			

Monday 3

Tuesday 4

Wednesday 5

"There is one great spectacle, grander than the sea, that is the sky; there is one spectacle grander than the sky, that is the interior of the soul."

VICTOR HUGO (1802–1885)

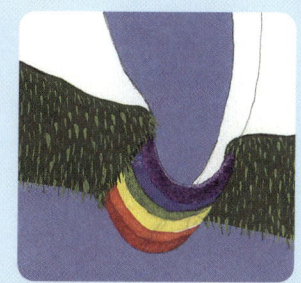

Rainbow bridge

A rainbow is a pledge of benign beauty, inspiring us with a sense of nature's variety – even, at times, with wonder. It shows us the way to cross the chasm of our limitations. But there will always be two magical colours missing – gold and silver. These we must find for ourselves, in the process of realizing our vision, empowered by the knowledge that even the best we can imagine falls short of the true miracles this life can offer us.

Thursday 6

Friday 7

Saturday 8
Bodhi Day (Buddha's Enlightenment) in some countries
Hanukkah begins at sundown

Sunday 9

December 10 – December 16

NOVEMBER							DECEMBER							JANUARY						
SU	M	TU	W	TH	F	SA	SU	M	TU	W	TH	F	SA	SU	M	TU	W	TH	F	SA
					1	2	1	2	3	4	5	6	7			1	2	3	4	5
3	4	5	6	7	8	9	8	9	**10**	**11**	**12**	**13**	**14**	6	7	8	9	10	11	12
10	11	12	13	14	15	16	**15**	**16**	17	18	19	20	21	13	14	15	16	17	18	19
17	18	19	20	21	22	23	22	23	24	25	26	27	28	20	21	22	23	24	25	26
24	25	26	27	28	29	30	29	30	31					27	28	29	30	31		

Monday 10

Tuesday 11

Wednesday 12

"Life is always a tightrope or a feather bed. Give me the tightrope."

EDITH WHARTON (1862–1937)

The art of balance

Transformation is a committed gesture of welcome to a new way of living – one that is in tune with our destiny and purpose. However, having recognized the change within ourselves, we must not expect it to be always visible. Life is a balancing act, and no radical change will ever make the tightrope wider. It's simply that we can now carry out our tricky manoeuvres with more joy and more conviction.

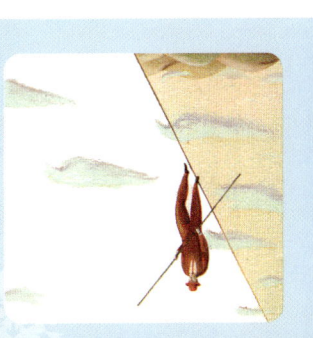

Thursday 13

Friday 14

Saturday 15

Sunday 16

December 17 – December 23

NOVEMBER

SU	M	TU	W	TH	F	SA
			1	2	3	4
5	6	7	8	9	10	11
12	13	14	15	16	17	18
19	20	21	22	23	24	25
26	27	28	29	30		

DECEMBER

SU	M	TU	W	TH	F	SA
					1	2
3	4	5	6	7	8	9
10	11	12	13	14	15	16
17	18	19	20	21	22	23
24	25	26	27	28	29	30
31						

JANUARY

SU	M	TU	W	TH	F	SA
	1	2	3	4	5	6
7	8	9	10	11	12	13
14	15	16	17	18	19	20
21	22	23	24	25	26	27
28	29	30	31			

Monday 17

Tuesday 18

Wednesday 19

"Everyone knows the utility of usefulness, but no one knows the utility of uselessness."

CHUANG TZU (4TH CENTURY BCE)

Panda power

Given that pandas are black and white, as well as Chinese, it is difficult to think of a better creature to represent the Tao – that is, the natural order of existence in ancient Chinese thought, often expressed as the sum of yin and yang, of all complementary opposites. Think of this creature as encompassing male and female and embracing all races. Buy a panda soft toy to give to a friend as the physical manifestation of cosmic harmony.

Thursday 20 ☽

Friday 21
Winter Solstice

Saturday 22

Sunday 23
Sun in Capricorn

December 24 – December 30

NOVEMBER

SU	M	TU	W	TH	F	SA
						1
2	3	4	5	6	7	8
9	10	11	12	13	14	15
16	17	18	19	20	21	22
23	24	25	26	27	28	29
30						

DECEMBER

SU	M	TU	W	TH	F	SA
	1	2	3	4	5	6
7	8	9	10	11	12	13
14	15	16	17	18	19	20
21	22	23	**24**	**25**	**26**	27
28	**29**	**30**	31			

JANUARY

SU	M	TU	W	TH	F	SA
				1	2	3
4	5	6	7	8	9	10
11	12	13	14	15	16	17
18	19	20	21	22	23	24
25	26	27	28	29	30	31

Monday 24
Christmas Eve

Tuesday 25
Christmas Day

Wednesday 26
St Stephen's Day, Boxing Day (Holiday: UK, Republic of Ireland, Australia, New Zealand)

"Dancing is the loftiest, the most moving, the most beautiful of the arts, because it is not mere translation or abstraction from life; it is life itself."

HAVELOCK ELLIS (1859–1939)

Dance of winter

Winter is often seen as the time of stasis – the pause when the life-force rests and gathers strength. Humans, however, are exempt from the requirement to hibernate. To show that your energy is undiminished, devise and perform a solo dance as a spell to keep wild creatures and vulnerable humans warm and safe in the harshness of winter weather. Let each movement you make be a prayer of compassion.

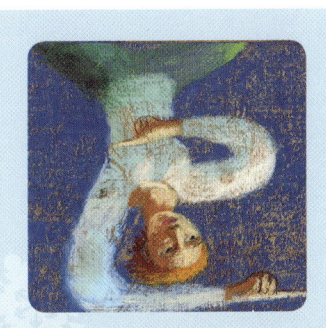

Thursday 27

Friday 28

Saturday 29

Sunday 30

December 31 - January 6

NOVEMBER

M	TU	W	TH	F	SA	SU
				1	2	3
4	5	6	7	8	9	10
11	12	13	14	15	16	17
18	19	20	21	22	23	24
25	26	27	28	29	30	

DECEMBER

M	TU	W	TH	F	SA	SU
						1
2	3	4	5	6	7	8
9	10	11	12	13	14	15
16	17	18	19	20	21	22
23	24	25	26	27	28	29
30	31					

JANUARY

M	TU	W	TH	F	SA	SU
	1	2	3	4	5	6
7	8	9	10	11	12	13
14	15	16	17	18	19	20
21	22	23	24	25	26	27
28	29	30	31			

Monday 31
New Year's Eve

Tuesday 1
New Year's Day
(Holiday: UK, Republic of Ireland, Australia, New Zealand)

Wednesday 2
Holiday
(Scotland, New Zealand)

❄

"When you get up in the morning, think of what a precious privilege it is to be alive – to breathe, to think, to enjoy, to love."

MARCUS AURELIUS (121–180 CE)

Start the year running

So 2012 did not bring apocalypse after all! Offer a prayer of thanks. Take a deep breath and throw yourself into the New Year with gusto. Don't bother with resolutions this time: you have already committed to a transformed self and a better world, so just enjoy the holiday, then afterwards continue to pursue your destiny as you previously intended. May your path shine bright and clear!

Thursday 3

Friday 4

Saturday 5

Sunday 6

Don't miss out on next year's diary, order your copies from September 2012, by phone or by post with FREE postage and packaging.*

Book of Days 2013 (254 x 185 mm) £12.99 (inc. VAT)
Pocket Book of Days 2013 (150 x 110 mm) £6.99 (inc. VAT)

Call Duncan Baird Publishers on 0207 454 8513 or send a cheque made payable to Duncan Baird Publishers (Reader Offers), 6th Floor Castle House, 75-76 Wells Street, London W1T 3QH.

"An ideal gift for thoughtful people of all ages – just be careful that you don't like it so much, you decide to keep it for yourself!"

Prediction Magazine

* Free postage & packaging for UK delivery addresses only.
Offer limited to 3 books per order.